The Story Comes Alive

A Guide to Experiencing Movies and Characters at Walt Disney World

VOLUME ONE

WALT DISNEY AND THE FAB FIVE

Trisha Daab

Theme Park Press

The Happiest Books on Earth

www.ThemeParkPress.com

Editor: Bob McLain
Layout: Artisanal Text

ISBN 978-1-68390-188-4
Printed in the United States of America

Theme Park Press | www.ThemeParkPress.com
Address queries to bob@themeparkpress.com

This book is dedicated to everyone who has read and supported me with my first two books. From local fans that go to every event and bring Girl Scout cookies, to friends and family who are not Disney fans but read my books and leave reviews. To fellow Disney fans from Connecticut to Tennessee to Texas to the UK. It is all of you that make writing about Disney possible. Thank you for being magical.

Contents

Introduction

My son loves Mickey, where can I find him at Disney World?
Daisy is my favorite character, where can I see all the Daisy stuff?
I want to honor Walt Disney. Can I see everything Walt in one day?

Does this question sound familiar? If yes, you're reading the right guide.

Whenever people ask me to help them with planning their Disney World vacation, the most common questions I get are: 1. Should I stay on property? (Yes; see my first book, *The Not-So-Evil Stepmother.*) 2. Where should I eat? (Lots of places; see my second book, *Tasting the Magic.*) And 3. How do I find Mickey, *Toy Story*, Ariel, [insert your favorite movie or character's name]? That's what this book is about.

A Character Meet & Greet should be on your list, of course, and will be in this guide. Also in this guide are many other magical experiences to add to your list of ways to see your favorite story come alive. When you are at Disney Parks, you get to go inside the stories—from rides and restaurants that feel like you are in the movie, to resorts with movie-themed rooms, to the hidden magic the Imagineers have sprinkled in everything from candy apples to wallpaper.

Character Meet & Greets are fun. There are hugs, autographs, and stories of evil stepmothers and sea witches. But there is so much more. How about singing along with your favorite character in a show? Or seeing a statue of them that is so big you can climb on it? Or making a cake that resembles a certain famous Mouse? This guide will tell you everywhere to experience the movies and characters you love including:

- Character Meet & Greets
- Attractions
- Shows
- Special events and festivals
- Resorts (Yep! There are movie-inspired hotel rooms.)
- Shops
- Dining and so much more!

My hope is this book will be like having a personal tour guide take you around Walt Disney World and help you see your favorite Disney stories come alive. And if you have a fun fact or a way *you* make that story come alive at Disney World that's not here, share it and tag #TheStoryComesAliveWDW and maybe you'll see it in a second edition!

We have never lost faith in family entertainment—stories that make people laugh, stories about warm and human things, stories about historic characters and stories about animals.

—Walt Disney

How to Use This Guide

With four parks, Disney Springs, two water parks, 23 resorts, two miniature golf courses, and other amenities, Walt Disney World (WDW) is the largest Disney resort with many ways to showcase characters and movies and truly bring the story to life. And there are A LOT of beloved characters and favorite movies and franchises in the Disney collection. We have captured a lot, but not all, of them in this guide. One of my kids even asked about including *Lizzie McGuire*, a 90s Disney Channel fave. Sadly, she did not make the cut.

Disney has a lot of movies. Any guesses on how many? 100, 500, 1000? According to D23, with the release of *Incredibles 2*, Disney has 733 films. Now not every one of those 733 films has a ride or show or a character you can hug and get their autograph at WDW. But, there a lot that do. And they are at WDW in a variety of magical ways.

Because there are so many magical movies and characters to experience, this is a series of five volumes. Which volume contains your favorites? See "Other Books in the Story Comes Alive Series" at the end of this book for more info. In this volume you will find:

- Walt Disney
- Mickey Mouse
- Minnie Mouse
- Goofy
- Donald (and Daisy) Duck
- Pluto

At Walt Disney World there are so many ways to see a story come alive. To make it easier to find the experience you're dreaming of, I've separated these different experiences into the following groups:

- Character Meet and Greets
- Character Meals, Dining, and Treats
- Rides/Attractions
- Shows, Parades and Dance Parties
- Nighttime Shows and Dessert Parties
- Statues, Fountains, Mini-Golf, and Other Semi-Permanent Fixtures
- Games
- Shops/Merchandise/Character Boutiques
- Special Events, Tours and PhotoPass Shots
- Mickey's Parties
- Epcot Festivals
- Resorts
- Seasonal
- And sometimes... a Sprinkling of Pixie Dust

To keep this from being Webster's Dictionary length, the descriptions in the chapters named after a character or movie are brief. But hakuna matata (no worries)! You can find detailed descriptions including times, locations and other helpful planning tips in the Appendix: How to Use This Guide Extended Version.

The beginning of each chapter will have all the different ways to experience your favorites in each of the categories above. This way you can read about the different meet and greets and decide which one or four to visit. Or read about the different resorts with a Mickey vibe and decide which is the right one for you.

Some movies and characters have so many things to see in each park that I added a little extra help. At the end of their chapter there is a checklist by park and Disney Springs. The list is a helpful way to plan your day in each park. And, if you're anything like me you love checking stuff off a list! How many items on your favorites list have you already experienced?

Did you know if you look in the My Disney Experience app late at night it says: Shh...Characters are Sleeping. That app and over 30 other sources from YouTube channels to books to interviews with Disney experts were used to try and bring you the most complete guide possible. Please make sure to check out the acknowledgments section for the complete list and to meet the experts interviewed. Who knows, you may just find your next favorite Disney blog or podcast!

One more thing...

Walt Disney dreamed of a place that kids and adults alike could play and imagine, a place that would always be changing. Where imagination comes alive.

Disney Imagineers are always dreaming. Thinking of new ways to sprinkle pixie dust and make a trip to any Disney Park magical. This means that no two trips to Walt Disney World are the same.

While all that Imagineering can reduce the chance of getting bored, it can also mean things that we love and cherish may change. Disney is sprinkling a lot of construction pixie dust lately and there are many new attractions, resort renovations, and changes underway.

While I have done many a late night of research on Disney's website and regular checks on the My Disney Experience app, there may be some details in this guide that have changed by the time you are reading it. They may not be getting rid of Cinderella Castle or Mickey waffles anytime soon, but character meet and greets are a place where Disney likes to mix things up. Menus are updated, parties and festivals tend to change every year and merchandise is always refreshed. Also, special events are often for a short time only. They may only be for one summer, with only some elements or characters returning.

If there is someone that you absolutely must see, stalk the My Disney Experience app, check the times guide when you arrive at the park, or as Disney blogger Serena suggests, "if you can't find a character that you're looking for you can always stop by guest services. They have a master list that they can look up and find out if they are appearing in any of the parks that week." Must see characters may take some persistence. It took me three trips before I finally caught the Evil Stepsisters from *Cinderella*. It was totally worth it.

Which stories are your favorites? How do you see those stories come alive while at Walt Disney World? Please share with me on Instagram @notsoevil_disneystepmom or Facebook @authorTrishaDaab. I love hearing from fans and, who knows, we may need to do another book with your requests!

CHAPTER ONE

Walt Disney

Walt Disney World and all of the magic Disney brings into the world would not have been possible without the imagination, determination and passion of Walter Elias Disney. Walt would say, "it was all started by a mouse." But really where it started was with a man who was full of ideas and dreams and the sprit and fight to make sure they came true.

Walt Disney died before Walt Disney World opened its gates. But his influence, his magical touch, is all around the Walt Disney World Resort. Disney has done much to honor Walt Disney throughout the parks and here is a brief guide to those places. Thankfully there are no character meet and greets.

One of the best ways to experience and honor Walt is to spend a day in the Magic Kingdom taking the time to notice the attention to detail and the care to providing a magical experience for kids and grown-ups alike.

Rides/Attractions

Magic Kingdom has three attractions with Walt Disney in the name. You won't see Walt but these are rides that have that vintage Disney feel. Make sure to ride and see every one.

Walt Disney loved trains and stated he wanted a train in every Disney Park. At Magic Kingdom you can take a ride on Walt Disney Railroad with stations on Main Street USA, in Fantasyland and in Frontierland. Not only can the train get you from one end of Magic Kingdom to the other, giving your aching feet a break, but it also has narration and provides interesting information on the history of the park and inspiration for the different lands in the Magic Kingdom.

It's not just the train ride that is magical; each station has its own way of seeing the story of Walt's love of trains. In the stroller area of the train station on Main Street pictures of Walt Disney riding his own backyard train have been spotted. At the train station in Frontierland if you go upstairs and pick up the phone, you can hear Morse Code of Walt's Disneyland opening day speech. The train stop in Fantasyland is near Storybook Circus. The restrooms near this train station are even themed like a train roundhouse.

Walt Disney's Enchanted Tiki Room is in Adventureland and features a room of audio-animatronic birds ready to serenade you. Like most attractions with Walt Disney in the name, it's an opportunity to sit down. It's almost as if Walt knew that guests would need an opportunity to sit, relax and cool down.

Like many of the attractions in your Walt tour of Magic Kingdom, Enchanted Tiki Room has a history with Walt and it was a Disney first. This attraction at Disneyland was the first show ever to use audio-animatronics. Let's take a moment to think about Disney World without audio-animatronics. There would be no pirate swinging his hairy leg, no country bears playing the banjo, and no yeti on Expedition Everest. A newer version of this technology is also used on the Frozen Ever After ride at Epcot.

"it's a small world" in Fantasyland may not have Walt Disney in the name but this attraction is based on an original idea from Walt Disney for the New York World's Fair. It features the artwork of Mary Blair, a Disney Legend and iconic artist who created concept art for many Disney films. (There is also a massive Mary Blair mural at the Contemporary Resort.)

Walt Disney's Carousel of Progress in Tomorrowland is an original Walt Disney creation. Like it's a small world, it was also created for the World's Fair. Also like small world, it has music that you hear repeatedly and that sticks in your head. Is it a "great big beautiful tomorrow" or "a small world after all"? You're welcome.

One of the best places in all of Disney World to learn about Walt is at Walt Disney Presents in Animation Courtyard at Hollywood Studios. The attraction tells the story of Walt and his legacy through art, video, and exhibits. This a self-guided walking tour in an air-conditioned space. One of my favorite parts of Walt Disney Presents is the model of upcoming Disney park additions from parks around the world. Disney's model's are incredibly detailed and even include miniature landscaping.

None of the attractions on this list have a height restriction, which is perfect, as Walt wanted kids of all ages to be able to enjoy Disney parks. Only "it's a small world" has FP+ and at this time none have a ride photo. The rest maintain that vintage Disney feel.

I can't leave out Animal Kingdom when talking about Walt. Walt Disney had a deep love of animals and wildlife. Many believe he would enjoy how the Imagineers have blended storytelling, animals, imagination, and conservation at Animal Kingdom.

Dining and Treats

Walt was a man with simple tastes and chili was one of his favorite foods. At Casey's Corner in Magic Kingdom there are famous foot long hot dogs and you can even get one with chili and cheese. Casey's is also known for its cheese sauce and the chili and cheese come on fries too. It's likely the stop Walt would have made for lunch.

50's Prime Time Diner on Echo Lake at Hollywood Studios is like being transported to an episode of *Leave it to Beaver* or *Dick Van Dyke*. Throughout the restaurant are different rooms that make it seem like you're dining right in the kitchen while Mom whips up her specialties. Walt loved Mickey and he loved Macaroni and Cheese. While Walt probably wouldn't be making a reservation at Victoria & Albert's he would like the family favorites served at 50's Prime Time Diner. In the Sampling of Mom's Favorites you get fried chicken, meatloaf, pot roast and mashed potatoes all on one plate.

But what makes this restaurant truly the place to go for Walt fans are the TVs at most of the tables. They show commercials from the 1950's, footage of Disneyland from back in the day and most exciting, an excerpt from Walt's speech at the opening day of Disneyland. Make sure to ask for a table with a TV when you check-in for your reservation.

DCP Anna shares a hidden drink connection to Walt at Trader Sam's Grogs Grotto at the Polynesian Resort:

> This is a little bit of a deep Disney Nerd dive, but I love the Rosita's Margarita at Trader Sam's. Trader Sam's is a not-so-secret secret bar at the Polynesian resort. It's tiny and intimate with seating for only about 50 people. In Walt Disney's Enchanted Tiki Room, there is a little throwaway line in the main song. Jose asks, "I wonder whatever happened to Rosita." This is an interesting question that Disney park fans have been asking themselves over the years. Was she one of the showgirls? Did she wind up on a lady's hat, like an old lyric from the same song suggests? Adding to the lore of this hidden story is a Tiki room showgirl seashell with the name "Rosita" that hangs from the ceiling in Trader Sam's. Trader Sam's represents a lot of what I love about Disney Parks. Everything is driven by story.

Nighttime Shows

For many years black-and-white footage of Walt appeared in the nighttime show at the Magic Kingdom, Wishes. In 2017 Disney debuted a new show called Happily Ever After. Though I miss seeing and hearing Walt, this new show is practically perfect in almost every way.

> *Tip*: You can create a Walt experience in Happily Ever After. Stand in the park area in front of Crystal Palace and Casey's Corner. During parts of the show, the Partners statue featuring Walt and Mickey will be in your line of sight. At times during the show it looks like the pair are standing in the doorway of the castle. Especially during the intro it seems as if the Imagineers planned for this, as Walt's wave almost seems part of the show.

Disney Movie Magic at Hollywood Studios is a spectacular celebration of Disney movies from *Mary Poppins* to *Guardians of the Galaxy*. The show opens with audio and video of Walt Disney sharing a few of his famous quotes. It's a moving tribute to Walt and is one of those moments that may give you the tingles. Toward the end there is a quote from the movie *Saving Mr. Banks*, starring Tom Hanks as Walt Disney. Fingers crossed with the opening of Toy Story Land in 2018 and Star Wars Land in 2019, this show will remain in the rotation of nighttime shows at Hollywood Studios.

With the new nighttime shows slated to open in 2019 (Wonderful World of Animation at Hollywood Studios and Epcot Forever at Epcot), I expect there will be at least one homage to Walt.

Statues, Streets, and Other Semi-Permanent Fixtures

To take in all the Statues, Streets, and other Semi-Permanent fixtures that will connect you to Walt the best place to start is in Magic Kingdom in Town Square at the Roy Disney and Minnie Mouse bench. Roy Disney, Walt's brother, was as important as Mickey Mouse or Walt himself to making Disney what it is today. Roy Disney did the official opening of Disney World and Magic Kingdom in 1971, dedicating the park to Walt. This bench has sculptures of Roy and Minnie sitting next to each other. The statues are positioned in a way that you can sit down with the two on the bench.

After taking your photo with Roy and Minnie, walk down Main Street and see all the tributes to Walt, the Imagineers and Disney legends in the windows along Main Street. The street was inspired by Walt's childhood home of Marceline, Missouri. There are a few windows honoring Walter Elias Disney. The first is on the train station as you enter the park. The next is at Fire Station 71. Last is the window above the Plaza Restaurant where Walt's window overlooks Cinderella Castle.

Continue your journey along Main Street and into the hub area in front of Cinderella Castle. At the end near the hub there is a statue called the Partners statue, where Walt and Mickey stand hand in hand looking at the crowds coming down Main Street with Cinderella Castle in the background. This is a popular PhotoPass spot.

Before you finish your Walt tour down Main Street make sure to gaze longingly at the castle and think about the Cinderella Castle Dream Suite, which was originally planned to be a special apartment for Walt and his family. Now, finish your tour of the Walt rides and attractions and then head to take the monorail over to Epcot.

Epcot or as Walt used to say Experimental Prototype Community of Tomorrow, was one of Walt Disney's ideas that he sadly did not get to see brought to life. Epcot is a true testament to the respect and admiration the Imagineers had for Walt and their dedication to continuing his dream even after he was no longer part of this world.

Before entering the park, take a trip on the monorail through it and admire the layout. A sketch Walt drew in 1966 inspired the whole idea. See a photo of Walt with the model for Epcot and explore the timeline of the park near, not in, Club Cool. There is a set of sliding glass doors before you go into Club Cool. Go through those doors and look for the big blue wall.

Thankfully this next group of semi-permanent fixtures is truly that, semi-permanent. There are few things that make a Disney fan shudder more than the word refurbishment. It's a necessary evil to keep Disney World feeling new and sparkly but there is one benefit, Walt Disney quotes on construction walls.

Yep. Disney is embracing the #wallsofdisney photo trend with the bubble gum wall, the popsicle wall, the famous purple wall but also with making the refurbishment walls a fun photo op. Most refurbishment walls include quotes from Walt and are designed to fit the land they are in.

"It's kind of fun to do the impossible" looked as if it was written on notebook paper by Andy in the walls near Toy Story land at Hollywood Studios prior to its opening in the summer of 2018. Fantasyland construction had regal purple plaques and "I only hope that we never lose sight of one thing – that it was all started by a mouse." The walls at Epcot surrounding the construction for the new Guardians of the Galaxy ride have a space theme and dark blue plaques with the Epcot logo, and futuristic white lettering with the Walt quote, "Most of my life I have done what I wanted to do. I have had fun on the job."

Shops/Merchandise

Ye Olde Christmas Shoppe in Liberty Square in Magic Kingdom has a special tribute to Walt's paternal grandfather. The story behind the store is that a German immigrant owns it and the family lives above the shop. There is a sign in the upper window of the home that says Kepple. This is in honor of Walt Disney's paternal grandfather Kepple Elias Disney. After looking for the window make sure to pop inside the shop for an ornament or the free smells of pine and cinnamon.

Walt appears on a fairly limited amount of merchandise. The best Walt souvenir is one of the many amazing books about Disney history or biographies of Walt. Books can actually be somewhat tricky to find but there are usually a few at the Emporium shop at Magic Kingdom and in the resort shops. There are sometimes book signings at Disney Springs. On Disneyworld.com search merchandise events to find information on authors or artists.

There is a Partners statue line of merchandise that includes a Pandora charm, a shirt and a hat. Not being a hat wearer, I still think it's the best piece in this line. It's dark blue with a white embroidered castle and the Partners Statue in blue in front of it. Let's hope this line lasts, as it really is a classy way to include Walt on merchandise. Products in this line have been found at Emporium shop at Magic Kingdom and Mickey's of Hollywood in Hollywood Studios.

Another location that you may be able to find Walt on artwork is at the Art of Disney shop at Epcot or Disney Springs. Pieces at this shop are typically limited editions and are priced as investments. If you purchase an item from this shop, I highly recommend considering the Disney shipping service. Disney will pack up your collectible and ship it directly to your home. It's reasonably priced and with insurance it's far more likely your precious Disney art will make it home in one piece.

One of my favorites is a black and white poster of Walt drawing Mickey while a full color animated Mickey is peeking at the drawing. It includes my favorite Walt quote, "I hope we don't lose site of one thing – it was all started by a mouse."

Tours

Walt Disney: Marceline to Magic Kingdom Tour is a must for fans of Walt Disney and the history behind how Disney became the kingdom it is today. Your knowledgeable tour guide will take you behind-the-scenes of classic attractions like those I mentioned in the Rides & Attractions section. These tour guides also have little-known facts about Walt, his upbringing and his magical touches on Walt Disney World that they will share during this 3-hour walking tour. The tour is geared more towards adults so you must 12+ to take the tour. The cost is actually fairly affordable for a Disney tour at $49 per person, but the price can change. The tour is only offered on certain days. You definitely need to make a reservation.

If you want to go even further behind the scenes try the Keys to the Kingdom tour. This tour also features stories about Walt but is a bit more about seeing the infamous Utilidors, the tunnels running under Magic Kingdom. This tour is a 5-hour walking tour and is for guests 16 and older. The cost has been around $99.00 and reservations are recommended. Photography is prohibited so come to learn and watch in wonder, not to flood your social media. This is a very cool tour but if you were looking for the tour that really focuses on Walt, I'd recommend the Walt Disney: Marceline to Magic Kingdom tour.

The Magic Behind our Steam Trains Tour at Magic Kingdom gives guests a rare peek into the Disney World roundhouse and the trains that Walt loved so much. During the tour the guides will talk about the role of trains in the parks and Walt's lifelong love of trains. This tour is for guests 10 and older and takes 3 hours. Cost: $54, subject to change. Reservation needed: Yes.

Resorts

Pictures of Walt can be particularly tricky to find at Walt Disney World. One surprising spot to find one is at the All-Star Movies Resort in the lobby.

There is also a photo of Walt and his wife Lillian ready for a luau on the first level of the Polynesian. It's down a hallway past the BouTiki store towards Capt. Cooks.

The Carolwood Pacific Room at Wilderness Lodge has rare photos of Walt Disney, train memorabilia and even a model train on loan from the Disney family. This is not a hotel room but a sitting room anyone can visit.

Theme park author Alexa thinks:

> Animal Kingdom Lodge just screams "Walt Disney" to me. When trying to create the Jungle Cruise attraction in Disneyland, he wanted real animals instead of the animatronics we have today. However, it just did not work out. Animal Kingdom Lodge, with real animals, cast members from African villages, authentic food and designs, everything about it seems like something Walt would have loved.

I agree with Alexa and believe Walt would like the story of the railroad behind the new in 2018 Copper Creek Villas and Cabins at Wilderness Lodge. One of the Imagineers involved with the project, Mitch, shares the new villas and cabins are "focusing on the railroad and focusing on Walt's love for the railroad. The Cabins would have been those of the supervisors and managers of the railroad and quarry."

On the design, Mitch shares it's "using found objects around the site to bring the outside in." There is a railway beam detail in the kitchen, a natural stone fireplace and a beautiful stunning piece of rock with swirling colors and a slight sheen that feels like you are on the inside of a cave. I think Walt would appreciate the simplicity of the design, the importance of the story, the railroad inspiration but also the thoughtful attention to detail.

Seasonal

Family was of the utmost importance to Walt Disney. He saw the holidays as a time for family and being together. So many Disney movies feature Christmas scenes because it was a time of year for magic and Walt loved bringing that magic to his family and to the world. At the Walt Disney Family Museum in California there is even an exhibit called *Home for the Holidays at Carolwood* celebrating Disney family Christmases. Walt would probably have loved Disney World every day every season of the year but Christmas would be that much more special.

Sprinkling of Pixie Dust

A World of Magic: Every Disney park, except Shanghai Disneyland, has it's a small world attraction. Every park has a slightly different interpretation of the ride with the original at Disneyland in California. The attraction at Disneyland in California also gets an amazingly detailed overlay every year for the Christmas holiday. Some experts expect that Shanghai Disneyland will be like Hong Kong Disneyland and the attraction in Shanghai will be added at a later date.

History of Magic: Country Bear Jamboree is an attraction for guests of all ages with a history of Walt and laughter. The story goes that Walt was visiting an Imagineer who was working on an audio-animatronic musical. Walt saw the concepts of a bear with a tuba and started laughing, a lot. A few days later, sadly, Walt Disney passed and Imagineers tell it that this bear with his tuba gave Walt his last good laugh. This story has been passed down to generations of Imagineers as Walt's Last Laugh. The Country Bear Jamboree was one of the last attractions Walt helped develop before he died. These bears and Walt's laughter now live on in this timeless attraction at Magic Kingdom.

Mickey Mouse

Mickey Mouse is a very tired mouse at the end of his day at Disney World. He gives a lot of hugs at the many Character Meet and Greets and meals, has quite a few wardrobe changes and even battles a huge snake every night in Fantasmic! at Hollywood Studios. He also hosts a number of Halloween and Christmas Parties every year. He is one busy mouse!

Mickey and his signature shape are all over Disney World. There are Mickey-shaped treats, paintings, sculptures at resorts and hundreds of hidden Mickeys. That Mickey shape has been around since the mouse was created in 1928 and is actually one of the most well-known icons in the world.

To experience most things Mickey and his iconic shape at Disney World would mean days, possibly even weeks at Walt Disney World. There are entire books devoted to just finding all the Hidden Mickeys so those concealed mice are not included in this guide.

What's here are more than 35 ways to find your magic with the Mouse. Mickey is hands down the character you can engage with the most with 9 character meet and greets and meals, 10 attractions and shows and 13 resorts where Mickey has statues at pools, in gardens and is even inlaid in marble. Are you up to the challenge? How many of these Mickey's can you check off the list?

Character Meet and Greets

NEW IN 2019
Meet Mickey Mouse and Minnie Mouse, Magic Kingdom

Mickey and Minnie are celebrating their 90th birthdays together at this meet and greet in Town Square Theater on Main Street. The space is party ready with streamers, balloons, and special outfits designed just for this event. Mickey has on a white suit sprinkled with confetti that totally makes me think of funfetti cake. Disney has said this Meet and Greet is temporary until September 2019. We shall see, but if it does end, you can still meet Mickey at Town Square Theatre, he just may not be wearing the funfetti suite anymore. And yes, even with those famous gloves, Mickey gives autographs. FP+: yes and recommended during busy times.

Meet Classic Mickey, Epcot

Meet Mickey at the Character Spot in Future World at Epcot. Mickey is typically in his traditional suit with red pants and bright yellow bowtie at this meet and greet. The background is a futuristic painting. FP+: yes and recommended.

Meet Sorcerer Mickey, Hollywood Studios

Meet Sorcerer Mickey at Red Carpet Dreams on Commissary Lane at Hollywood Studios. Mickey is in all his Fantasia Sorcerer glory at this meet and greet. He has the blue Sorcerers Hat covered in white stars, the flowing red robe and the backdrop has the famous spell book and even a broom. Thankfully this broom has not come alive. Make sure you take your time to check out all the cool lighted posters as you walk down the hallway to the meet and greet. FP+: no. This is one of the only Mickey meet and greets that does not have a FP+. Now that was at the time of publishing and Disney loves to change stuff like that as soon as someone puts it in a book.

Meet Safari Mickey, Animal Kingdom

Meet Mickey in his Safari Gear at the Adventurer's Outpost on Discovery Island at Animal Kingdom. Mickey is channeling his inner Indiana Jones in safari shirt and brown shorts with a totally Indy-looking hat. The background is a mural representing the different areas of Animal Kingdom, including a dinosaur skeleton. Why choose this meet and greet? Because you get Mickey and Minnie TOGETHER. This is actually more difficult to achieve than you might think. This is one of the Mickey meet and greets that closes the earliest, sometimes at 7:30 PM, depending on how busy the park is. FP+: yes and recommended because this mouse can always draw a crowd.

Character Meals, Dining, and Treats

Chip n' Dale's Harvest Feast, Epcot

Mickey. In overalls. Yep. Farmer Mickey is a regular at Chip n' Dale's Harvest Feast at Epcot. This character meal at the Garden Grill Restaurant in the Land Pavilion is an all-you-can-eat family-style meal for breakfast, lunch, and dinner. The restaurant spins so that you can see different parts of the Living with the Land attraction while you are dining. Oh, and your vegetables at dinner are grown in that attraction. Reservations: highly recommended. Arrive early and ask to sit on the lower level to get one of the booths.

Minnie's Seasonal Dine, Hollywood Studios

Minnie has the honor of hosting a meal for each season in Hollywood Studios and Mickey is an honored guest. All of the characters costumes change each season and there are some spiffy spring, summer, Halloween and Christmas costumes. Get all the details of the meal in Minnie's Character Meals or just get the scoop on Mickey's threads at these meals in Seasonal.

Safari Character Meal, Animal Kingdom

It's another Safari Mickey, this time a little less Indiana Jones inspired and with a side of Mickey Waffles or curry chicken. Tusker House in Africa at Animal Kingdom is a character meal buffet with Mickey, Donald, Daisy and sometimes Goofy, but with a twist. In addition to the standard Mickey Waffles and bacon, Tusker House has offerings with African flavors. This is DVC Sarah's favorite character meal because "the breakfast food is the best!" For breakfast there are Mickey waffles and Jungle Juice and lunch and dinner include multiple curries and basmati rice. Not feeling adventurous? There are also scrambled eggs or Corn Dog Nuggets, but what better place to try something new than at a buffet? With a mouse in a safari hat and a duck in khaki colored heels (referring to Daisy, not Donald.) Reservations: highly recommended.

Ohana Character Breakfast, Polynesian Resort

Stitch waffles. I think Stitch would really like waffles. The menu at the Ohana Character Breakfast at the Polynesian only lists Mickey waffles, but Stitch waffles have also been spotted. What people really love about this breakfast is meeting Lilo, Stitch, Hawaiian Mickey and sometimes Hawaiian Pluto. Like all character meals, there's no guarantee who will be there but Lilo and Stitch are pretty much a given.

Lilo is in her signature red dress with a lei and pretty red flower in her hair. Mickey is wearing a shirt with a similar red and white pattern as Lilo's dress with a lei and white pants. Not sure why, but this look on Mickey was really giving me a dad vibe. Pluto and Stitch are in their leis. Meals served: this is breakfast only. Ohana is open for dinner, but at the time of publication, it is not a character meal. Reservations highly recommended.

Chef Mickey's Character Meal, Contemporary Resort

Chef's Mickey, Minnie, Donald, Goofy and Pluto are all coming out of the kitchen for photos and autographs at Chef Mickey's at the Contemporary Resort. Mickey is in his chef's hat and a there is artwork all around the restaurant for more great photo ops. There is even a small Chef Mickey statue as you are coming into the restaurant. Characters may vary, but these five are typically standard. You can ask when checking in which characters will be around. Meals served: breakfast, brunch and dinner. All are buffet. Reservations highly recommended. This is one of the more difficult reservations to get and this meal is very popular. If you are over at the Magic Kingdom, you can just walk to the Contemporary.

Tip: Though an excellent character meal and one of the rare places to have the Fab 5 together, it is also very loud and very busy. If you're looking for more great Mickey photos, check out the Mickey neon wall outside the Bay View Gifts shop.

TOP TEN MICKEY-SHAPED TREATS

🐭 MICKEY ICE CREAM BAR. Find this legendary Disney treat just about anywhere around Walt Disney World. Sprinkled around all the parks are freezer carts and the resorts have them in the stores. One of my favorite photos of my son during 18th birthday trip to WDW was his breakfast of cotton candy in one hand a Mickey bar in the other. Disney breakfast of champions. DCP Anna once saw one thrown against the Expedition Everest mountainside at the highest point of the coaster.

🐭 MICKEY PRETZEL. Yes there are the hard little pretzels but this Mickey pretzel is the warm chewy pretzel that's the size of a small child's head. Just look for the food carts with the warmers.

🐭 MICKEY WAFFLE. You'll find these at pretty much every breakfast buffet. Short on time? Find them at the ice cream shop on Main Street in Magic Kingdom until early lunchtime. Can't get enough Mickey waffles? Mickey waffle makers are available for purchase online or at Mickey's Pantry in Disney Springs.

🐭 MICKEY APPLE. One more way to enjoy a different treat for every season. There is actually a year of candy apples, with a new apple to try for each month of year. Mickey as a leprechaun, a jack-o-lantern, and a snowman are just a few of your tasty options.

🐭 LARGE KRISPY HEAD. This is a Mickey-shaped krispy treat that is so huge the label literally says Large Krispy Head. Hee hee. Now there are small normal human sized krispy treats in the shape of Mickey too. However you will know when you have found the Large Krispy Head, as it will likely be larger than *your* head. In some locations they even have an impression of Mickey's face in them. These are the perfect souvenir for the sweet tooth back home and can be found at most bakeries including Main Street Confectionery in Magic Kingdom.

- MICKEY COOKIE. My personal favorite is the charming gingerbread man during the holidays. It's a typical gingerbread man shape but with Mickey ears.

- MICKEY CUPCAKE. Disney gets how much we all love cupcakes and there are a few different Mickey varieties that have been seen at the bakeries around Disney World. One of the most popular is the Oreo cupcake at the Boardwalk Bakery at the Boardwalk Resort. This cupcake is topped with white frosting red crunchie balls and a full Oreo cookie decorated to look like Mickey with icing red pants.

- MICKEY GELATO. Head to L'Artisan des Glaces in France at Epcot for an ice cream or sorbet with a special treat. Ask for the Mickey macarons and they will add two little macarons perfectly placed to look like Mickey ears to your ice cream or sorbet. The macarons come in different colors and flavors. It's just a few dollars more for this *tres magnifique* photo-worthy dessert. And depending on the time of day, the display case will have the ice creams scooped into a Mickey shape. Disney is all about those details.

- MICKEY CAKE AND SANTA MICKEY CAKE. Buy it or make your own at Amorette's Patisserie at Disney Springs. These cakes look as good as they taste, which is not always the case for Mickey desserts. For those with serious dessert goals or who are visiting with a group and a lot of forks you can buy a whole Mickey cake. There are also individual-size Mickey pastries. You can also take a class at Amoretti's for $149 for up to 2 people (prices subject to change) and make your own scrumptious mouse concoction. This includes beverages, including those of the grown-up variety. There are classes to make the classic Mickey cake or a seasonal offering on Monday and Wednesdays. Reservations: yes and highly recommended.

MICKEY CAKE POP. These come in a variety of styles. At Main Street Confectionery in Magic Kingdom there is a 1-2 bite-sized intricately decorated cake pop decorated just like your favorite mouse. There are also larger versions covered in dazzling sprinkles in a variety of colors. Our AP expert Jamie has a tasty photo of one of the purple ones in front of the purple galactic wall in Magic Kingdom.

Rides/Attractions

Mickey's PhilharMagic, Magic Kingdom

Mickey's PhilharMagic in Fantasyland at Magic Kingdom is an epic 3D movie experience with many favorite Disney movie classics. There's music, a carpet ride with Aladdin and Jasmine, Donald being shot out of a tuba and the smell of apple pie. Philharmagic should be on your list. FP+: offered but not usually necessary. No height restrictions or ride photo but there is a great photo op with a Donald statue in the shop at the exit of the show.

Carousel of Progress, Magic Kingdom

Mickey appears in multiple forms in the classic Disney attraction Carousel of Progress in Tomorrowland at Magic Kingdom. See if you can spot them all! There is one Mickey in the 1940s Halloween scene and there are five in the final Christmas scene. This is the perfect ride to rest your feet and maybe even your eyes. FP+: no and not needed. Height restrictions: none

Living with the Land, Epcot

Know a gardener that loves Mickey? Then a relaxing trip on the Living With the Land attraction at Epcot is a must if you want to see giant Mickey-shaped pumpkins and topiaries. FP+ yes but not typically needed unless the park is at the highest crowd levels. Height restrictions: none. Ride photo: not an official one but have a camera handy to capture all Mickeys.

> *Tip*: grab a healthy bite at Sunshine Seasons
> in the land pavilion to taste some of the fresh
> veggies, fruits and herbs you saw on the ride.

Mickey and Minnie's Runaway Railway, Hollywood Studios

This ride is slated to open in 2020 and will have the honor of being the first Mickey-themed ride-through attraction. This ride is replacing the Great Movie Ride. It is inspired by the Mickey shorts that have appeared on the Disney Channel and features a new animation style. The ride will completely immerse you in a cartoon world where Goofy is a train engineer. That should only ever happen in a cartoon. You board Goofy's train and go on a wacky ride. The attraction will have a new short and song created specifically for the ride.

Shows, Parades and Dance Parties

Let the Magic Begin, Magic Kingdom

Let the Magic Begin is a 5-minute stage show with multiple characters there to welcome you to a magical day at the park. It happens most days before Magic Kingdom opens. During the show Mickey will welcome you to the park in his traditional costume.

If you're already up early, see the show. It's sweet, quick and with a simple storyline that even the littlest of kids or the Dug in your group can make it through without getting bored. There are princesses, a prince, Pluto and even a few evil stepsisters. It's quite the mix of characters and they are really able to show off their personalities

Festival of Fantasy Parade, Magic Kingdom

Mickey and Minnie close out the parade in a beautiful hot air balloon float. Mickey is feeling very "Greatest Showman" in a multicolor top hat, red ringleader jacket and blue pants.

Mickey's Royal Friendship Faire, Cinderella Castle, Magic Kingdom

During this 22-minute show you can see Mickey donning some Shakespearean style garb and singing and dancing with most of his Fab 5 friends and a few princesses and princes from faraway lands.

Move It! Shake It! MousekeDance & Play It Street Party, Magic Kingdom

This show has the unique honor of being a parade and dance party all rolled into one. Mickey has on his party gear and hangs out on float during the party dancing. Mickey has invited a whole host of friends including Minnie, Donald, Goofy, Chip and Dale. Mickey stays on his float during the parade but other characters wander around and dance with guests that are hanging around the area in front of the castle.

Disney Jr. Dance Party, Hollywood Studios

You've given Mickey hugs, seen him in pumpkin form and eaten some Mickey shaped treats but now it's time to dance with Mickey at the Disney Jr. Dance Party in Animation Courtyard at Hollywood Studios. This show made its debut in the fall of 2018 and kids of all ages can dance and sing along with Doc McStuffins, Vamparina, Mickey and Timon. The show is very interactive, is a great way for little ones to burn some energy dancing and singing along and for parents to rest their feet and maybe even their eyes. FP+: yes. Height restrictions: none.

> *Tip*: This show is really geared towards smaller children. If you have a moody teen or tween maybe send them to Trolley Car Cafe (aka Starbucks) while you check out the show with your young ones.

Nighttime Shows

Fantasmic!, Hollywood Studios

In 30 minutes you will get to see Mickey do four costume changes, control water, lasers, battle a snake and a dragon and heroically perform some magic. You'll see traditional Mickey in his red pants, a white top and sparkly black tuxedo style jacket. He also wears his old fashioned blank tank with red shorts, dons a red robe and the blue sorcerers hat and my favorite, when Mickey is DisneyBounding as Snow White.

Okay well he's not officially DisneyBounding Snow White but in the scene when he is battling the dragon (aka Maleficent) Mickey is wearing yellow pants, a red cape and a blue shirt. One of the best moments of the show is when Steamboat Willie appears piloting a black and white ship with over 30 colorfully dressed characters.

In the show there are also clips of Mickey in *Fantasia* and placed into other Disney classics like *Aladdin*. Come for the Mickey and stay for the pyrotechnics, lasers, and storytelling and to see what Disney can do with a million gallons of water.

NEW IN 2019!
Wonderful World of Animation, Hollywood Studios

This new show slated to open in May will be projected on the Grauman's Theatre. Disney describes it "as a journey through more than 90 years of Disney and Pixar animation." Like Walt was famous for saying, "it was all started with a mouse," the show starts and ends with Mickey.

NEW IN 2019!
Epcot Forever, Epcot

Opening in fall of 2019 to replace Illuminations. It is not confirmed that Mickey will be in it, but is worth checking out.

Lightning Rods, Golf Courses, and Other Semi-Permanent Fixtures

The Partners Statue in the Hub area at Magic Kingdom. This area is popular for photos day and night and you can often find a PhotoPass photographer nearby.

Mickey was at the opening of MGM Studios (now Hollywood Studios) on May 1, 1989 and left behind some Mickey glove prints in the forecourt of Grauman's Chinese Theatre at Hollywood Studios. Mickey is also at the top of Crossroads of the World in Hollywood Studios. This is not just for decoration. Mickey's ear is grounded and he serves as a lightning rod.

The store Mickey's of Hollywood at the same park has a statue of Sorcerer Mickey in the hat, red robe and with a few brooms with buckets. If you're not able to make it over to Red Carpet Dreams to meet an actual Mickey in this get up, this is a decent photo substitute.

See one of the most clever Hidden Mickeys in Africa at Animal Kingdom. This Mickey is on a wall in Africa and has a unique look. Near him it says says Fichwa Fellow. In Swahili, "fichwa" means hidden.

See a Mickey topiary outside one of the entrances to World of Disney at Disney Springs. He tends to be decorated for the season with colorful flowers in spring and a festive Santa hat during the holiday season.

Is Sorcerer Mickey your favorite? You can see multiple statues of him and most of the characters from *Fantasia* at the Fantasia Gardens miniature golf course. The entire course is *Fantasia* themed with dancing hippos, a row of brooms with buckets and even a hole inside an ice cave. There are a ton of photo ops at this course and it's open most days of the year when weather permits. There are usually coupons and discounts available online or ask the concierge at your resort. The course is in the Epcot Resort Area. Busses are offered.

Would you rather see Mickey covered in snow or as a jack-in-the-box? Then head to the winter course at the Winter Summerland mini-golf course. Get on your Disney ugly Christmas gear and head over to this mini-golf course. There is a winter side course and a summer side course. There are more Mickeys on the winter side. Make sure you take your time at the Defrosty the Cooler hole to see a gingerbread Mickey. You can also see Mickey covered in snow with his pals Minnie and Pluto near the merry moguls hole. It's open most days of the year when weather permits. There are usually coupons and discounts available online or ask the concierge at your resort. Just hop on the bus towards Blizzard Beach.

If you prefer your golf in the non-miniature style, see Mickey-shaped bunkers at multiple golf courses around Walt Disney World. For more than 40 years there has been a Mickey-shaped bunker at the Magnolia course and in 2018 Disney has announced more Mickey bunkers are coming.

Games

Each time you play Sorcerers of the Magic Kingdom you receive a new pack of cards. There are over 70 different cards including, Apprentice Mickey's Broomsticks and Mickey's Magic Beans. There are special cards during Mickey's Not-So-Scary Halloween Party and Mickey's Very Merry Christmas Party. Go to the Firehouse on Main Street USA to play.

Shops/Merchandise

Disney is a merchandising machine and it all started with when a man approached Walt Disney at a hotel in New York City in 1929 and asked him if he could pay Walt $300 to put Mickey Mouse on a pencil. In 2017 the retail sales in Disney consumer products division was $1.5 Billion. Nice job Walt.

TOP TEN MICKEY SOUVENIRS

- MICKEY STICKY NOTES. The mouse will help you stay organized with colorful Mickey heads and Mickey-shaped food sticky (Post-It) notes. This is a souvenir that I have on multiple trips said: "I need this." And am quite happy I did. It's more fun to make notes to yourself on a Mickey cookie. Except you don't use them for fear of running out so then they just sit there looking cute and delicious.

- MICKEY FASHION. Shirts, flip flops, pants, sweatshirts, dresses, skirts, socks, ties, boxers, jewelry, even rompers. There is enough Mickey clothing at Disney World to let you create an entire wardrobe and go a month without wearing the same thing twice. There is even underwear for kids and boxers for men. Many useful items as long as you're not hanging with Disney haters. And if you are, that's the time to wear the Disney underthings.

- MICKEY HOUSEHOLD/KITCHEN GOODS. Tongs, dish-towels, sheets, cookie jars...the list goes on. It's another category of keepsakes that can actually be quite useful.

- MICKEY ORNAMENTS. If you have a Christmas tree and decorate with ornaments this will be a magical reminder of your Disney vacations every holiday season. Ornaments can make a great souvenir to get each trip and depending on how often you go, you may amass quite the collection. Ornaments are also a thoughtful gift for a Disney fan. With five kids giving Disney-themed gifts at various holidays and multiple trips to Disney with a souvenir ornament from each, our Christmas tree is a magical mix of castles, characters and confections.

🐭 MICKEY PLUSH. Every Disney household needs a soft, floppy Mickey plush. They are great for hugs, they pull together a Disney display and are a perfect photo prop. Our Mickey has been passed down from one kid to another and has been so loved one of his ears is coming off.

🐭 MICKEY PINS. There is a pin for everything. Epcot Festivals have pins. Mickey's Halloween and Christmas Party have special pins. There are pins for Disney Vacation Club (DVC) members and pins for Annual Passholders. There's a pin for just about every movie, character, show, attraction, idea, friend, Imagineers dog, well maybe not that last one but there are Slinky Dog pins. Mickey is a staple in the world of pins. Next time you're at a rack of pins see if you can find at least 10 pins that include Mickey Mouse.

🐭 MICKEY EARS. These ears come in so many different shapes, sizes and styles. You have the famous bride and groom and graduation ears and the traditional Mickey and Minnie Ears. There are seasonal ears: orange sequin Halloween ears with a black bow with orange polka dots and sparkly ears with a mini Santa hat for Christmas. And it gets even more interesting. Then there's the Lion King Animated Glow Headband. Say that 10 times fast. The latest are the Made with Magic line that include LED lights in the ears and the light will change, blink and pulse along with the music in nighttime shows. I have more ears than I will ever wear and look absolutely ridiculous in them all. Some people look great in them. I am not one of those people. Yet I still have 5 pairs that are only ever worn at Disney World and local Disney events and—seeing as I live in Chicago—that's maybe three times a year.

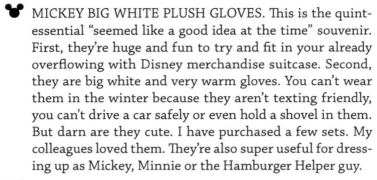 MICKEY BIG WHITE PLUSH GLOVES. This is the quint-essential "seemed like a good idea at the time" souvenir. First, they're huge and fun to try and fit in your already overflowing with Disney merchandise suitcase. Second, they are big white and very warm gloves. You can't wear them in the winter because they aren't texting friendly, you can't drive a car safely or even hold a shovel in them. But darn are they cute. I have purchased a few sets. My colleagues loved them. They're also super useful for dressing up as Mickey, Minnie or the Hamburger Helper guy.

MICKEY LIGHT UP SPINNY THINGS. This is the souvenir that every parent is pained about buying. Well every parent except DVC Dawn, "we like to spend our money on light up toys that end up annoying everyone around us" For the rest of us, you know as you are opening your wallet to get the cold hard cash or Disney Visa that a few hours from now you will be undoubtedly carrying this item into your resort because your child forgot it on the bus and because it cost so darn much, you grabbed it for them.

MICKEY BALLOONS. This is a souvenir I can't get behind. Yes they are cool but it is the most short-lived not-at-all useful souvenir. Unless you are doing a photo shoot. Save the $9-$14 and buy a pair of underwear or a pack of post its.

Most if not all of the souvenirs in this list can be found at one of the shops along Main Street in Magic Kingdom, the main gift shops in other parks, many resort gift shops and World of Disney in Disney Springs.

Mickey's Birthday, Marathons, and PhotoPass Magic

Every year in November Disney World does something to celebrate Mickey's birthday. In the past there has been free special ear hats and buttons. But in 2018 the party is going big because the mouse is turning 90! The party kicked off with a 3-day celebration at Magic Kingdom in November of 2018 where guests sang "Happy Birthday" to Mickey and danced with Mickey in the Hub or over at Tomorrowland.

When you turn 90 Disney goes all out and they are doing that with the World's Biggest Mouse Party. This is being celebrated at all the Disney parks and the Disney Cruise Line and will be at Disney World in 2019. The Walt Disney World celebration includes special merchandise like a Mickey celebration sipper; special Mickey's 90th Birthday stickers you can get free from cast members; the new Mickey and Minne meet and greet; and all new costumes for Mickey and Minnie seen in parades and shows. This celebration is being reported as only going until September 2019, but as you have seen throughout this chapter, there are a lot of ways to celebrate the mouse.

At the Walt Disney World Marathon, Mickey hosts the marathon and gets sporty in a coach outfit. He is on the medal for the marathon and the 2018 medal even had a spinning feature. You might see King Mickey cheering you on at the Disney Princess Marathon. At the *Star Wars* Marathon sometimes Mickey as Luke visits from far, far away. At the 2018 Wine & Dine Marathon Chef Mickey in his bright red chef coat and white chef's hat was featured at the event and on the medal. Mickey can also be seen in his overalls and checked shirt at the Fall Fest 5K.

Mickey has a bit of PhotoPass magic to add to your Disney pictures. In the past, in front of the train station at Magic Kingdom and on Main Street there has been a Mickey balloon Magic Shot. At Hollywood Studios in front of the arch outside Star Wars Launch Bay I've had a magic video with Mickey in a top hat and cane strolling and whistling while Pluto pops in and sits in a chair. There has also been Mickey sitting on a bench in Epcot.

While at Disney Springs, pop over to the PhotoPass Studio to find virtual backdrops. There has been one for Mickey and the Roadster Racers. Just tell the PhotoPass photographer that you love the mouse and they will hook you up.

Mickey's Annual Parties

They are his parties so obviously you will see a lot of the mouse at these events. At Mickey's Not-So-Scary Halloween party he is out of his normal wear and dressing up for the festivities in a costume. Most of the costumes can be best described as Halloween Mickey and usually involve an orange and purple jacket, vest and pants and a top hat. There always seems to be a top hat in his costumes. Mickey wears the costume in his meet and greet at the party and again in the parade. He rides in a float with Minnie and a few of his costumed friends.

Mickey shows up again in the form of treats. The treats tend to change up every year but the Mickey Pumpkin cheesecake is one that foodies want to see on the menu again. He is also all over the merchandise. Mugs, popcorn buckets, shirts, pins, there is a whole lot of Halloween mouse.

If you prefer your souvenirs free just grab some party maps. They are everywhere and always have Mickey in some sort of design on the cover. They are a cheap way to brag to your friends about the party. Or be like crafty AP Jamie and put the map and the decorative party wristband in a shadow box.

The holidays are about spending time with the ones you love, and Mickey and Minnie do just that for Mickey's Very Merry Christmas Party and the party-exclusive merchandise. Most years there are shirts, Magic Bands, pins, and an ornament only available for purchase during the party. The 2018 design had Minnie and Mickey under the mistletoe and a design with Mickey in a giant pile of gifts. Find these souvenirs at the Emporium, Ye Olde Christmas Shoppe, and Big Top Souvenirs.

You can't have a party without treats and Mickey has the Disney pastry chefs working hard every year to come up with sweets for his party. There's a cinnamon roll the size of a small child's head with red and green frosting in the shape of Mickey. Looking to put on your winter weight? Then go for the red velvet Mickey waffles. Grab a sweet treat and head to the windows of the Emporium to see statues of Mickey and his friends in *Mickey's Christmas Carol*.

The mouse loves a good ugly Christmas sweater and even has a fun photo backdrop for a Magic Shot during the party. At previous parties this has been near Ariel's Grotto in Fantasyland.

How many wardrobe changes do you think Mickey does at his Very Merry Christmas Party? Outfit one. Meet and get pictures with Mickey in his traditional Mickey costume with a few holiday touches. He has his red pants and black jacket but with a plaid scarf, vest, and merry green bowtie. Mickey is in his typical spot at Town Square Theater on Main Street.

Outfit two. Mickey and Minnie appear on a very festive float towards the beginning of the Once Upon a Christmastime Parade. Mickey's very jaunty in his plaid green jacket, vest and bowtie with cream-colored pants.

Outfit three. He appears in a different costume at the beginning of Mickey's Most Merriest Celebration Stage Show. At the end of the show is outfit four in five hours, Santa Mickey. Minnie and Mickey appear as Santa and Mrs. Claus at the end of the show.

Epcot Festivals

Mickey's topiary at the Flower and Garden Festival tends to move around and be a bit different every year. He is often right up in the front of the park in front of Spaceship Earth. He's been holding flowers for Minnie, a sorcerer in the scene from Fantasia and in a Hawaiian scene holding a shell. Mickey is always on some sort of merchandise for Flower and Garden and there is usually a theme that has Mickey with another character. He's appeared on flowerpot shaped coffee mugs with Pluto, as a topiary on an event exclusive pin, and hung out in Mickey's Grove with Orange Bird.

Chef Mickey is not just a restaurant in the Contemporary resort! He is also a food-loving mouse that loves to pop up around the Food & Wine Festival. 2018 included a whole line of Chef Mickey festival merchandise from super cute plush to salt and pepper shakers and even a pie plate. That same year he was also one of the prizes for completing the Remy's Ratatouille Hide and Squeak. These prizes change and Chef Mickey has not been a prize every year. Definitely worth checking to see if you can get a fairly inexpensive Chef Mickey souvenir.

Resorts

Campground

Campers and cabin dwellers can see a statue of Mickey in a seasonal costume at Meadow Trading Post at Fort Wilderness. Mickey has been sporting his farmer look in spring and summer, a frontier look in fall and even a Santa costume with a Christmas tree in the winter.

Value Resorts

Sorcerer Mickey has his own fountain and is in control of the water in the Fantasia Pool at the All-Star Movies hotel.

At the All-Star Music and Sports Resorts they are getting you ready for the new attraction coming to Hollywood Studios *Mickey & Minnie's Runaway Railroad.* Head to the food courts to check out the different artwork that adorns the walls and even the booths at All-Star Sports. A Mickey poster is also the primary artwork in the rooms at All-Star Music. It has Mickey in a darkened theater conducing a colorful orchestra.

At All-Star Sports there is a Mickey statue. Mickey is also the symbol in the center of the football field in the Touchdown area of the resort. At the All Star Movies Resort in the refurbished rooms you can find a *Mickey & Minnie's Runaway Railroad* inspired art print with Mickey, Minnie and Donald in the room.

The Pop Century Resort has Mickey in a way you are not likely to see him anywhere else at Disney World, as a phone. And not one of them new-fangled mobile phones, Mickey is a giant multi-story rotary style phone in the 70's section at the Pop Century. I wonder if it makes that loud clicking sound the phone made as you dialed? A Mickey pop art print is the art seen in the rooms at the resort.

Moderate Resorts

Lounge on the beach with Pluto and Mickey on the fold down bed at Caribbean Beach Resort. When the bed is down there is a sweet painting that your little beach goer can enjoy as they drift into dreamland.

Deluxe Resorts and Villas

Mickey and Minnie have a nice quiet moment on the beach in the art print on the walls of the 1-bedroom suite at the Beach Club. Mickey sand dollars are the pattern on the shower curtain in the suite and standard rooms at the Beach Club. If you prefer your Mickey merchandise with a nautical theme, head over to the gift shop at the Yacht Club resort.

A Mickey topiary is holding the sign for the Disney Vacation Club area at the Wilderness Lodge Resort. Mickey is also in a totem pole with his friends Goofy, Donald and a bear at the Mercantile store in the lobby of the Wilderness Lodge.

Rest your park-weary head on a yellow throw pillow with Mickey's face on it at the Contemporary resort. The yellow is the color of Mickey's classic costume bow tie. Some rooms have this throw pillow and others don't so make sure to look at Disneyworld.com and check the room photos to make sure you get a room with it if this pillow is a must have.

Probably the second-best Mickey statue in Disney World is outside the Contemporary Resort in the back along Bay Lake. It's a metal statue of a Mickey sitting on the top of a Mickey head. There is even a camera stand that let's you do a timed photo with the family. Just outside the Bayview Gifts shop in the lobby you'll find one of the famous Disney photo walls, the Neon Mickey wall. This wall has an Andy Warhol vibe with a grid of multiple Mickey heads in different neon colors. Make sure to pop in an elevator at the resort to hear Mickey or one of his friends tell you which floor you are on.

Connected via a bridge to the Contemporary is Bay Lake Tower, a Disney Vacation Club (DVC) Villa resort. Bay Lake has Mickey carpeting lining the hallways, has a Mickey shaped splash pad and a very contemporary slide featuring a few neon Mickeys.

Bay Lake Tower rooms have art prints with a pop art style of Mickey, Goofy, and Minnie. The studio has a pop art poster of Mickey. The 1 and 2-bedroom villas have my favorite piece, a pop art style painting with colorful silhouettes of Mickey, Minnie and Goofy. In the 1-bedroom villa there is an additional piece with Mickey that is a drawing and is actually the same art seen on the throw pillow in some rooms at the Contemporary. In the 2-bedroom villa you get the pop art, the drawing and additional artwork over the beds in the second bedroom with Minnie over one and Mickey over the other.

A 1920s-style Mickey and Minnie are going for a ride in a classic car in the carvings on the back of the chairs in the rooms at the Boardwalk Inn. All of the rooms have a vintage style but very limited characters. Mickey has a love of magic and you can see magician Mickey at Magic Kingdom and I think he would really love the AbracadaBar at Boardwalk Inn. The space is completely magician themed with props from famous magicians, a magic filled cocktail menu and best of all are the bathroom signs. They are themed and quite clever.

Grand Floridian is home to a few Hidden Mickeys. See a not so hidden mickey in the marble floor near the entrance of the main lobby at the Grand Floridian.

Have a healthy budget for your next Disney stay? Then you can try the new resort coming in 2019 the Riviera Resort. This is a villa resort and more than 40 signature art pieces were created just for it. One of these pieces is Mickey and his favorite pup lounging at a resort in the actual Riviera on the rooms fold-down bed. The art varies by room and room type so ask a cast member when checking in.

Seasonal

In addition to hosting some very merry and not so scary parties at Magic Kingdom, Mickey dresses up and has some fun to celebrate every season. The most epic way to celebrate the Halloween and holiday seasons with Mickey at Disney is his parties at Magic Kingdom. If a party is not your thing, no worries there are other fun ways to enjoy Mickey every season.

Spring

If you're at Disney World around Easter and looking for some eggs to hunt, head to Epcot for the Egg-Stravaganza. Mickey has been one of the eggs to find and has had the honor of being one of the eggs you can win for completing the search.

From March to June Mickey is pulling out his dapper style at the Minnie's Springtime Dine at Hollywood and Vine at Hollywood Studios. Mickey has been seen sporting a pink blazer, vest and spiffy vintage shoes. If vintage style is your thing, definitely check out this Character Meal. Read all about this meal and the other seasonal dines in the "Minnie" chapter under "Character Meals."

Summer

June to September is beach time for Mickey at Minnie's Summertime Dine at Hollywood and Vine at Hollywood Studios. Mickey is beach ready in a bright yellow tee and beach shorts.

Fall/Halloween

Halloween season at Disney starts in September and runs to early November at Minnie's Halloween Dine at Hollywood Studios. Mickey's costume? I call it "preppy vampire."

Fall is all about the Mickey jack-o-lanterns. They are everywhere around Magic Kingdom. They're on light posts, as just giant decorations around the park and right as you are coming in. Pumpkin spice lattes, apple cider, caramel apples, candy corn and Mickey cinnamon rolls are all tastes of fall you can find around Disney World. And of course there is always some sort of Halloween inspired Mickey candy apple.

Holiday Season

Right after Halloween it's time for the holidays. In addition to hosting the Mickey's Christmas party, Magic Kingdom is the place any holiday Mickey fan should visit. There are decorations everywhere, special holiday merchandise, and even window displays with scenes from *Mickey's Christmas Carol*.

This is also the time of year for the Holiday Dine at Hollywood Studios that runs until early January. Of Mickey's four different costumes at these events, the Holiday Dine and springtime are my favorites. For the holidays, Mickey's festive red coat has buttons that look like peppermint candy.

No Disney fan's house is complete without Mickey and Minnie holiday merchandise. For the holidays Disney releases blind pin packs, adorable plush, shirts, dinnerware and of course ornaments. There are even ornaments for many of the different resorts. The Contemporary ornament in 2018 was Mickey and Minnie with a Mary Blair inspired look. You can find the resort holiday ornaments at that resorts gift shop and often at Disney Days of Christmas in Disney Springs.

Do you prefer your holiday Charles Dickens style? Head to Hollywood Studios during the holidays to see Sunset Seasons Greetings. There you can see scenes from *Mickey's Christmas Carol* on the billboards and then see the Tower of Terror transformed to a snowy Victorian-era holiday scene complete with candlelit windows. This includes the shadow of people hurriedly moving through the city to get home for the holiday. Can you spot Mickey and Minnie dancing in one of the windows? (You need to be on the side of the tower closest to the ride entrance to see them.)

Also at Hollywood Studios during the holiday season is the Jingle Bell Jingle Jam nighttime show. The show is on screens next to and projected onto Grauman's Chinese Theatre. The show is separated into different sections by classic holiday songs. You can see Mickey in scenes from *Mickey's Christmas Carol* and *Pluto's Christmas Tree* during the songs "Walking in a Winter Wonderland" and "Need a Little Christmas."

If you can't make it to Mickey's Very Merry Christmas Party and are looking for those festive pics, head to Animal Kingdom. It is the place with the holiday dressed characters. You can meet Holiday Minnie and Holiday Mickey in their matching sweater and Santa hat. This is typically at their Discovery Island location, but make sure to check the app, the times guide or ask a Cast Member for the location.

Every year Disney decorates for the holidays and the resorts are no exception. From early November to early January, Disney World becomes even more magical. If you have an extra few hours and want a break from the parks head over to the Epcot resorts area. At the Yacht Club Resort there is an incredible holiday model train set. Hidden on the backside of the train set from the main entrance of the lobby is Mickey's Village with Mickey building a snowman, Minnie and Pluto hanging out, Christmas trees with Mickey decorations, many Mickey snowmen and Mickey buildings, one of which is a Mickey's Ear Factory.

The Disney pastry chefs make resort lobbies around Walt Disney World smell of gingerbread for the holidays. These displays are a site to see and they smell amazing. The gingerbread house at the Grand Floridian has been a holiday tradition since 1999. The primary person you will see is Santa but if you look closely above the windows there is a festive Disney touch and Mickey has been known to be on there in a wintery scene.

A tiny chocolate Chef Mickey is hard at work in his holiday bakery making trays of treats, gingerbread houses and Christmas trees made of cookies. And no, this is not life size this is all miniature *inside* of the gingerbread house at the Boardwalk Resort. The attention to detail inside this gingerbread house is mind-blowing. There are trays of tiny treats, each one decorated and even a table with bags of flour. The theme may change up each year but you should definitely have the Boardwalk lobby as a stop on your tour of holiday resort decorations. From here you can just hop on the boat across the lake to Yacht and Beach Club to see even more.

If cake is on your wish list, head to Amorette's at Disney Springs for a Santa Mickey cake. Buy it or make your own. A class at Amoretti's costs $149 for up to 2 people per cake. This includes beverages, including those of the grown-up variety. Reservations: yes and recommended.

Once you have your Mickey cake, pop over towards the Disney Days of Christmas at Disney Springs to check out the holiday windows and then take a pic in a winter scene with Mickey, Donald, Goofy and Pluto. Then visit the new in 2018 Nostalgic Mickey and Minnie Christmas tree at the Disney Springs Tree Trail. Who has more decorations, Minnie or Mickey?

Sprinkling of Pixie Dust

More than 250. What do you think that number represents? Think, think. Merchandise? Nope. Mickey bars my teenage son eats on an average trip? Nope. It's the number of different costume outfits for Mickey. In this book alone there are 26 different outfits listed for this stylish mouse.

Free Mickey! As one of the icons of the park, Mickey is on stickers that cast members have on hand to give to guests.

Give a cast member a smile, ask them a question, or just say thank you to them for all the magic they create and they may share a little Mickey magic in return. This goes for most cast members too, not just those in the parks. Greeters and mouse-keeping at resorts, bus drivers and even custodian services have all shared a little sticker magic with me in the past.

> *Tip*: One of my favorite ways to get a Mickey fix is on the monorail. There's a fuzzy carpet thing behind the seats that has a Mickey head on it. (*AP Jamie*)

Can't wait to get into the parks to see Mickey? There's a charming backdrop just outside the Disney Earport store at the Orlando Airport. Not sure whether to call this a painting or a sculpture or a mural but whatever it is, it features Mickey with the icon for each of the four Disney parks. It's a 3D piece so Mickey can hold your favorite souvenir, or wear a pair of Mickey ears or even hold your favorite Disney guidebook.

> *Tip*: Send a letter or wedding invitation to Mickey and Minnie and they may just send you a cool postcard. (*Theme park author Alexa*)

The Magic of Mickey by Park

Mickey at the Magic Kingdom

- Meet Mickey, Main Street USA
- Mickey and Mickey Balloon PhotoPass Magic Shots, Town Square, Main Street USA and outside the park in front of the Train Station
- Get Mickey cards, Sorcerers of the Magic Kingdom Interactive Game, Main Street USA
- Mickey/Walt *Partners* Statue, Hub Area, Main Street USA
- Mickey in Let the Magic Begin show, Castle Forecourt Stage, Main Street USA
- Mickey in Mickey's Royal Friendship Faire, Castle Forecourt Stage, Main Street USA

- Mickey in Move It! Shake It! MousekeDance & Play It Street Party, Hub Area, Main Street USA

- Mickey in Festival of Fantasy Parade, Main Street USA, Liberty Square, Adventureland

- Mickey's Philharmagic, Fantasyland

- Sir Mickey's shop, Fantasyland

- See Mickey Plush and Posters, Carousel of Progress, Tomorrowland

- Mickey as a Jack-o-Lantern decorations & apples, throughout park during the Halloween season

- *Mickey's Christmas Carol* window displays, shops on Main Street USA, during the holiday season

- Mickey's Not-So-Scary Halloween Party, special dates during the Halloween season

- Mickey in Mickey's Boo-to-You Halloween Parade, Main Street USA, Mickey's Not-So-Scary Halloween Party, special dates during the Halloween season

- Mickey at Mickey's Very Merry Christmas Party, special dates during the holiday season

- Mickey in Once Upon a Christmastime Parade, Main Street USA, special dates during the holiday season

- Mickey in Mickey's Most Merriest Celebration show, Castle Forecourt Stage, special dates during the holiday season

Mickey at Epcot

- Meet Classic Mickey, Character Spot, Future World

- Meet Farmer Mickey at Chip n' Dale's Harvest Feast character meal, Epcot

- Mickey shaped vegetation, Living with the Land ride, Future World West

- Mickey Topiaries, during all 4 Epcot Festivals, typically near entrance of the park

🐭 Mickey eggs in Egg-Stravaganza, World Showcase, special dates in Spring

Mickey at Hollywood Studios

🐭 Mickey Statue/lighting rod, top of Crossroads of the World Building

🐭 Mickey in Fantasmic! Nighttime Show, Sunset Boulevard

🐭 Coming in 2020: Mickey and Minnie's Runaway Railway ride, and Mickey in the new nighttime show, World of Animation, Grauman's Chinese Theatre

🐭 Mickey handprints, forecourt of Grauman's Chinese Theatre

🐭 Mickey at Disney Jr. Dance Party, Animation Courtyard

🐭 Meet Hollywood, Springtime, Summer, Halloween and Holiday Mickey at Minnie's Seasonal Dine Character Meal, Hollywood and Vine

🐭 Meet Sorcerer Mickey at Red Carpet Dream, Commissary Lane

🐭 Mickey in Jingle Bell Jingle Jam nighttime show, Grauman's Chinese Theatre, during the holiday season

🐭 *Mickey's Christmas Carol* in Sunset Seasons Greetings nighttime show, Grauman's Chinese Theatre, during the holiday season

Mickey at Animal Kingdom

🐭 Meet Safari Style Mickey, Discovery Island

🐭 See Fichwa! Fellow Mickey wall, Africa

🐭 Meet Mickey at Safari Character Meal, Tusker House, Africa

🐭 Meet Holiday Mickey, Discovery Island, holiday season

Mickey at Disney Springs

- Mickey Dome Cake, Amorette's Patisserie
- Mickey virtual backdrop, PhotoPass Studio
- Mickey sculpture in a winter scene, outside Disney Days Of Christmas
- Santa Mickey Dome Cake, Amorette's Patisserie, holiday season
- New in 2018! Nostalgic Mickey and Minnie Tree, Disney Springs Tree Trail, holiday season

CHAPTER TWO

Minnie Mouse

Minnie, like Mickey Mouse, was created in 1928. She has appeared in more than 74 cartoons with Mickey, given hugs to millions of guests at Disney parks around the world and has become a global fashion icon.

Rock the Dots with Minnie is celebrated on January 22, National Polka Dot Day. This has included a very popular line of Minnie merchandise, special media events, and even an exhibition at the Paper Agency in LA.

Minnie Mouse has an honor not even bestowed on Mickey; she has a fleet of vehicles at Walt Disney World. That's right. If you need a ride at Disney World and are willing to pay, log onto Lyft and get yourself in a Minnie Van. These vans are perky Minnie Mouse red with giant white polka dots. They aren't cheap but if you want to get from one resort to another, hate waiting in lines for the bus or you just want to ride in a polka dot car with a clever name, this is the vehicle for you.

> *Tip*: Ask your Minnie Van driver about a transportation card. Just like the cards they give on the Disney busses and monorail, they have a Minnie Van card with information about the van. (*AP Jamie*)

Despite all this fame, Minnie remains a sweet, humble mouse who loves to give hugs and see how guests are showing off their own Minnie Style at Disney World.

Character Meet and Greets

NEW IN 2019
Meet Mickey Mouse and Minnie Mouse, Magic Kingdom

Mickey and Minnie are celebrating their 90th birthdays together at this meet and greet in Town Square Theater on Main Street. The space is party ready with streamers, balloons, and special outfits designed just for this event. Minnie has a fabulous polka dot dress that has a layered skirt filled with brightly colored pom pons. Disney has said this Meet and Greet is temporary until September 2019. We shall see, but if it does end, my hope is they will bring back the Magnifique Minnie at Pete's Silly Side Show. FP+ yes and recommended when the park is busy

Meet Minnie, Epcot

Meet Minnie in her signature red polka dots at the Character Spot in Future World at Epcot. If you're looking for the standard Minnie in a bow and polka dots with the bright yellow heels, this is the meet and greet for you. The background is a futuristic painting and doesn't quite match what we think of when we think of Minnie, but she will always have a big smile. FP+: yes and recommended.

Meet Movie Star Minnie, Hollywood Studios

Meet movie maven Minnie at Red Carpet Dreams on Commissary Lane at Hollywood Studios. Minnie looks very vintage Hollywood in her flowing pink gown, elbow length white satin gloves, pink bow and silver heels. That's right, silver heels. She is one elegant mouse. Minnie's backdrop has an old 20s Hollywood vibe with deep reds and gold accents. She even has a chair with a few films props that honestly look a bit cartoonish against the art deco style background. Love the chair? Get it in your shot. Agree with me and think it's out of place? Just angle your shot accordingly or ask the PhotoPass Photographer to place the shot so the chair is hidden! Make sure you take your time to check out all the cool lighted posters as you walk down the hallway to the meet and greet. FP+: not available.

Meet Safari Minnie, Animal Kingdom

Meet Minnie and Mickey TOGETHER at the Adventurers Outpost on Discovery Island at Animal Kingdom. Getting pictures with this mouse couple together can actually be pretty tricky. Definitely visit this location if a pic of the happy mouse couple is a must on your list or if you are super into safari chic. Minnie is sporting her safari gear with a brown shirt and skirt and even brown boots with a little kitten heel.

The background is a mural honoring all the different areas of the Animal Kingdom Park. But the coolest prop in this area is Minnie's blue and pink polka dot suitcase. Minnie may be setting aside the dots in her outfit but she has to always rock a few dots! The suitcase is over to the side so if you want it in your pic just ask the character to stand in an area so it's in the picture. This is one of the meet and greets that closes before the park, sometimes at 7:30 PM, depending on crowd levels. FP+: yes and recommended

Character Meals, Dining, and Treats

Minnie can actually be fairly tricky to find at a character meal. Surprised? Me too. If you're visiting during January or February, you'll have to venture over to a resort for lunch with Minnie. For the rest of the year there is Minnie's Seasonal Dine at Hollywood and Vine in Hollywood Studios. This meal typically happens most of the year with the Springtime, Summertime, Halloween and Holidays Dines for lunch and dinner and the Silver Screen Dine that is dinner only and runs from January to March. Check out Disneyworld.com for the exact dates for each season.

The menu, decorations and the special outfits worn by Minnie, Mickey, Goofy, Donald and Daisy change based on the season. This is the usual cast of characters but may be subject to change. When you're checking in ask who is at the party to manage any superfan's expectations. The meal is buffet style with unlimited trips and an extensive dessert section. During breakfast this location is host to the Disney Jr. Play and Dine. Reservations highly recommended.

Minnie's Silver Screen Dine, Hollywood Studios

At this dinner only event Minnie and her friends are all decked out Hollywood Glamour style. Goofy has a zoot suit vibe in his deep red jacket. Donald's going for the slick movie start look with a black leather looking jacket with a crisp white shirt and hat. Mickey looks sharp in his shiny blue tux with black bowtie. The hostess is sweet in shimmering bright pink dress with her signature Minnie bow but it's Daisy who really steals the show. With her feather hair piece, bright purple eyeshadow and dark gown Daisy is definitely giving off the dramatic starlet vibe.

The decor of the space already has an old Hollywood feel with pics of old Hollywood, a mural of a Hollywood map and art deco style carpeting. With the bright lights and noise of most character meals, Hollywood and Vine feels more loud movie set than elegant dinner party.

Speaking of dinner, let's talk food. Creamy popcorn soup garnished with caramelized popcorn, lobster and shrimp macaroni and cheese and sparkling cookies and cakes are items listed on this menu. Really, almost every dessert has some sort of silver or gold detail or sparkling sprinkles. So grab a gold cookie and diva it up with Daisy.

Minnie's Springtime Dine Character Meal, Hollywood Studios

Springtime Dine is all about the flowers, pastels and fresh tastes. Minnie and Daisy are sweet in their floral dresses and fancy bows. Mickey and the boys are quite spiffy in their springtime gear and all look like they're ready for Dapper Day with jackets, vests and vintage looking shoes. Mickey is even wearing a pink blazer! Now that's something you don't see every day.

The menu includes springtime tastes and flavors like corn, a soup and salad bar and Mickey's Must-Haves of fresh fish and roasted plantains. Ever wonder what ducks eat? Well Donald's Delectable Entrees section has included Mongolian Beef and Stir Fry Yakisoba noodles. There's even a children's buffet that is set at a child's level so they can fill their own plates with mini corn dogs, pasta and baked chicken.

Desserts? Oh yes. Daisy's Delightful desserts area has had chocolate and strawberry cupcakes and a chef's springtime creation. Dapper Day, dressing up and DisneyBounding with vintage styles is becoming huge. If vintage style is your thing, definitely visit this meal to see your favorite characters in their dapper styles.

Minnie's Summertime Dine Character Meal, Hollywood Studios

Ready to hit the beach? So is the crowd at Minnie's Summertime Dine. Minnie has a fun floral print and pink heels while Daisy has yellow heels and a fabulous summer hat to match her floral beach cover up. The boys are a bit more casual with Mickey in a t-shirt, Goofy in a vest and what looks like some red Chuck Taylors. And then there's Donald dressed for lifeguard duty complete with floppy hat and whistle.

The summertime menu has salads, lots of seafood options and the always-popular carving station. Summertime at Disney World can be full of fun, heat, lots of ice cream, humidity and exhaustion. This meal is an excellent way to cool off, check some characters off your list and refuel before taking on some Stormtroopers and Slinky Dog Dash.

Minnie's Halloween Dine Character Meal, Hollywood Studios

Halloween Dine has the characters dressing up for some tricks and treats. Minnie is the spider queen with cobweb tights, gloves and spider accessories. The decorations at this event are a bit on the light side but Minnie typically has a photo spot with a spooky neighborhood vibe backdrop. Daisy is with Minnie on the spider theme with an orange and purple dress and a Halloween purple bow. Donald is out of this world in a space costume and Goofy is a colorful Halloween-loving cowboy with a cowboy hat, purple pants, orange shirt and lime green vest. It's as colorful as it sounds, but it works.

Mickey's costume is a bit less direct but I think it may be preppy vampire? Purple striped pants and a purple checked vest with green shirt and shiny green shoes are topped off with a purple and green vampire cape. The characters really seem to have a fun time at this dine, playing hide and seek, dancing and having fun with guests.

The buffet is packed with fall flavors of pumpkin, sauces and a little hint of spice not seen in the summer or springtime dines. All of the food items have fun seasonal names and past dishes include: Hocus Pocus Pork Loin, Tombstone Taters, and the festive soups Bubbling Brews of Witches Vegetable Potion and Smoked Pumpkin Patch Soup. The desserts have been fall flavors with a Halloween theme: pumpkin cheese-cake, candy corn cupcakes and even treats with jack o lantern Mickey candies on top. If you have anyone in your group that has serious arachnophobia just make sure you prepare them in advance for the arachnid-inspired fashions!

Minnie's Holiday Dine Character Meal, Hollywood Studios

This is the meal to ring in the season. Santa Goofy greets diners at the door and Minnie is ready for the holidays in a sparkly red dress. Mickey is quite snazzy in his red coat that even has buttons that look like peppermint candy. Donald is channeling his inner Scotsman with a red check hat and vest. Yes, even during the holidays, Donald doesn't wear pants. And this time Daisy is *sans* pants too and is sporting a green tunic with sparkly snowflakes along the lace edging. The best is her festive red heels with a matching green bow.

The food is chock full of flavors of the season with cranberry butter with pretzel bread and cornbread stuffing and Cherry Port Ham and soup and oh, the desserts.

In the past there has been a chocolate fountain and in front of the fountain were two big festive cakes. One had a Minnie ornament atop of box of presents bursting with desserts. The other was Mickey trying to hold together a cake that split in two with even more sweet things inside. They look delicious, but you cannot have these cakes. But, there are so many cookies, pastries, and even chocolate covered marshmallows that you probably won't mind. Between hugging fancy dress characters and stuffing all the holiday chocolate in your face you can sing along with some holiday songs. And, if the festive rhythms get you, maybe even do a little dance.

Chef Mickey's Character Meal, Contemporary Resort

Chef's Mickey, Minnie, Donald, Goofy and Pluto are all coming out of the kitchen for photos and autographs at Chef Mickey's at the Contemporary Resort. Minnie is in her signature polka dots with a pretty apron. Characters may vary, but these five are typically standard. You can ask when checking in which characters will be around. Meals served: breakfast, brunch and dinner. All are buffet. Reservations highly recommended. This is one of the more difficult reservations to get and this meal is very popular. If you are over at the Magic Kingdom, you can just walk to the Contemporary.

> *Tip*: Though this is an excellent character meal and one of the rare places to have the Fab 5 together, it is also very loud and very busy.

Minnie's Beach Bash Breakfast, Beach Club Resort

Minnie, Daisy, Donald and Goofy are stopping off for a quick breakfast with you before heading to the beach. They are all dressed for a stylish day in the sand with Minnie in a straw hat, a shirt and shorts with sea horse detail and blue heels with yellow starfish. This character meal is breakfast only. It is at Cape May Café at the Beach Club Resort. The characters have stayed fairly consistent but it's always worth checking at check in before making any promises which of Minnie's friends will be at the beach bash. The meal is a buffet with standard breakfast options including Mickey waffles.

Tip: You can walk or take a boat into Epcot from this resort. Both options will have you entering via the International Gateway (between UK and France) in World Showcase.

Minnie Cupcakes, Multiple Locations

Can't make a meal and just need a little treat to get your Minnie fix? Head to one of the bakeries for a Minnie cupcake or cake pop. The elegant Rose Gold Minnie Mouse Ears cupcake at Sunshine Seasons at Epcot or the Millennial Pink Minnie cupcakes found at the All-Star and multiple other resorts prove that Disney will typically have on-trend treats. Seriously, there were four different types of millennial pink Minnie cupcakes around Disney World at one point. The version at Mara at Animal Kingdom Lodge even had fondant ears and edible glitter! What trend will we be munching on next?

Minnie Chocolates, The Ganachery, Disney Springs

During the Rock the Dot events on January 22, National Polka Dot Day, there is usually a special event at Disney Springs. During that time (and most of the year, really) you can find some sort of Minnie-inspired chocolate at The Ganachery. Around Easter beautiful chocolate domes stuffed with special surprises were topped with a pink chocolate Minnie-ear headband.

Rides/Attractions

Mickey and Minnie's Runaway Railway, Hollywood Studios

This ride is slated to open at Hollywood Studios in 2020 and will have the distinction of being the first Mickey-themed ride-through attraction.

This ride is replacing the Great Movie Ride and is inspired by the Mickey shorts that have appeared on the Disney channel and features a new animation style. The ride will completely immerse you in a cartoon world where Goofy is a train engineer. That should only ever happen in a cartoon. But it happens on this ride and you will get to board Goofy's train. The attraction will have a new short and song created specifically for the ride.

Shows and Parades

Let the Magic Begin, Magic Kingdom

Let the Magic Begin is a 5-minute stage show with multiple characters there to welcome you to a magical day at the park. It happens most days before Magic Kingdom opens. Minnie comes by in her signature red polka dot dress to help Mickey say hello to all their guests.

Festival of Fantasy Parade, Magic Kingdom

Mickey and Minnie close out the Festival of Fantasy parade in a beautiful hot air balloon float. Minnie's outfit is all kinds of fantastic. It's a red and yellow polka dot dress with a pink ribbon detail along the bodice, skirt and a pretty pink bow at the waist. She has a pink bow and sorcerer's hat with the same polka dot and ribbon detail as her dress. For part of 2019, Minnnie will wearing her 90th Birthday Celebration polka-dot dress during the parade.

Mickey's Royal Friendship Faire, Cinderella Castle, Magic Kingdom

Minnie and her friends are looking a bit "ye olde Fantasyland" in this 22-minute show. As always Minnie looks fabulous but is not rocking any of her signature polka dots. Minnie loves this show because she gets to meet Elsa. She's a big Elsa fan.

Move It! Shake It! MousekeDance & Play It Street Party, Magic Kingdom

This show has the unique honor of being a parade and dance party all rolled into one. Minnie has on her party gear and hangs out on float during the party dancing.

Nighttime Shows

Fantasmic!, Hollywood Studios

Fantasmic! is a unique nighttime spectacular at Hollywood Studios in a stadium that was specifically designed just for it. This jam-packed show has over 50 costumed performers who sing, dance and perform stunts on the rock formation set or on one of the many floats that glide by. There are different scenes over the course of the 30-minute show from Mickey's dreams of dancing princesses and happy elephants, to the invasion of the villains that give Mickey nightmares of snakes and dragons.

You will see over 15 Disney films projected on walls of water, cheer on Mickey as he battles a glowing dragon and snake, see fireworks and wave at over 30 live characters from a wide range of films on a boat piloted by Steamboat Willie.

Minnie is there at the end to help Mickey celebrate defeating the villains in his nightmares.

NEW IN 2019!
Wonderful World of Animation,
Hollywood Studios

This new show slated to open in May will be projected on the Grauman's Theatre. Disney describes it "as a journey through more than 90 years of Disney and Pixar animation." Since Minnie has been a Disney staple in Disney animation since 1928, I expect she will be in this show.

NEW IN 2019!
Epcot Forever, Epcot

Opening in Fall 2019 to replace Illuminations. It is not confirmed that Minnie will be in the show, but is worth checking out.

Statues, Handprints, Mini Golf, and Other Semi-Permanent Fixtures

Minnie has a special bench in Town Square at Magic Kingdom. Minnie is sitting with Roy Disney and there's room for one more and a memorable photo.

Minnie has a small statue in the hub area in front of Cinderella Castle at Magic Kingdom. The statue is bronze and Minnie is of course in her signature bow.

Minnie and her favorite mouse Mickey were at the opening of MGM Studios (now Hollywood Studios) on May 1, 1989 and left behind some handprints in the forecourt of Grauman's Chinese Theatre at Hollywood Studios.

Minnie is playing in the snow over at the Winter Summerland mini-golf course. Get on your Disney ugly Christmas gear and head over to this mini-golf course. There is a winter side and summer side. Minnie is over on the winter side hanging out with Pluto and Mickey near the merry moguls hole. The course is open most days of the year when weather permits. There are usually coupons and discounts available online or ask the concierge at your resort. Just hop on the bus towards Blizzard Beach.

Shops/Merchandise

Like her main mouse Mickey, Minnie is on a lot of merchandise. You can find something with Minnie on it, has polka dots like Minnie, bows like Minnie wears or is just straight up a dress so you can look just like her. Since there are so many options, here are a few that stand out.

Let's start with Minnie ornaments in many shapes, sizes and styles. Every Disney fan with a Christmas tree should have at least one Minnie ornament. Go park-lover style with Minnie and Mickey in different scenes inspired by all four parks. Rock the dots with a glass ball with a pink or red polka dot bow.

Be festive with Mickey and Minnie arm in arm dressed for the holidays. Minnie even has red shoes with a green bow. Speaking of shoes... For the person that can never have enough shoes there is a Minnie shoe ornament and a Minnie handbag ornament. All of the ornaments can be personalized and found at Ye Olde Christmas Shoppe at Magic Kingdom or Disney Days of Christmas at Disney Springs.

Disney is really getting on the DisneyBounding bandwagon with the clothing lines Oh My Disney, Get Into Character, and all the 50's inspired dresses, skirts and accessories that started appearing with the 2017 opening of the Dress Shop at Cherry Tree Lane at Disney Springs. For Minnie fans, you can now get adorable rompers with polka dot shorts and a bow belt and a polka dot halter dress. The best shops for harder-to-find more fashion-forward souvenirs is Keystone Clothiers at Hollywood Studios and the Dress Shop at Cherry Tree Lane at Disney Springs.

Do you love taking selfies at Disney? So do Daisy and Minnie. They even have a pin of them doing a selfie in front of the castle. Find it at most pin shops at the parks and resorts.

Marathons and PhotoPass Magic

At the Walt Disney World Marathon Minnie hosts the 10K and gets sporty in a coach outfit with a pleated skirt. She also sometimes appears on the medal and the 2018 medal even had a polka dot ribbon. You might see Princess Minnie cheering you on at the Disney Princess Marathon. At the *Star Wars* Marathon sometimes Minnie as Princess Leia visits from far, far away. At the Wine & Dine Marathon Minnie can sometimes be spotted wearing a beautiful Italian-inspired costume or her apron over her polka dot dress as Chef Minnie. Minnie can also be seen in her overall dress and checked shirt at the Fall Fest 5K.

Minnie has a bit of PhotoPass magic to add to your Disney pictures. Near Town Square at Magic Kingdom, look for a PhotoPass Photographer near one of the benches. They often don't have a tripod. There is a super sweet magic shot where a cartoon Minnie will be added in to sit next to you on the bench.

Mickey's Annual Parties

As the mouse's leading lady Minnie is always on the guest list. Minnie has beautiful costumes for Mickey's Not-So-Scary Halloween party at Magic Kingdom. Unlike Mickey, Minnie's is always pretty clearly a friendly witch or princess.

She is on the float with Mickey in the parade, has a meet and greet in her costume, had her own party-exclusive witch cupcake at the 2018 party and is often on the merchandise with Mickey. One of the pieces of party merchandise from 2018 I am coveting is the pin set that was characters with treats. Minnie is dressed as a sparkly Halloween cupcake in front of a backdrop of cupcakes and she even has sprinkles on her bow.

Minnie tends to get festive with Mickey for the Mickey's Very Merry Christmas Party exclusive merchandise. Most years there are shirts, Magic Bands, pins and an ornament that is only available for purchase during the parties. The 2018 design had Minnie and Mickey under the mistletoe. Find most of the party souvenirs at the Emporium Shop, Ye Olde Christmas Shoppe and Big Top Souvenirs.

Grab a sweet treat and head to the windows of the Emporium to see statues of Mickey and his friends in *Mickey's Christmas Carol*. Minnie appears in the window for one of the last scenes when the Cratchit family is celebrating Christmas morning.

How many wardrobe changes do you think Minnie has at Mickey's Very Merry Christmas Party? Let's count them.

Number one, meet and get pictures with Minnie and Daisy. These ladies are ready for a holiday party. Minnie is wearing an elegant satin dress with candy stripes on the skirt.

Outfit two. Mickey and Minnie appear on a very festive float towards the beginning of the Once Upon a Christmastime Parade. Minnie is in a fancy red dress with a cream jacket and shiny red heels.

Outfit three is my favorite. In the Mickey's Most Merriest Celebration show Minnie starts the show in a party perfect skirt that looks like a decorated Christmas tree. Bringing her to out four in five hours, Minnie and Mickey appear as Santa and Mrs. Claus at the end of the show.

Epcot Festivals

Minnie's topiary at the Flower and Garden Festival tends to move around and be a bit different every year. She is often with Mickey and right up in the front of the park in front of Spaceship Earth. One of my favorites was the year they had Minnie and Mickey replicating American Gothic with Mickey holding a pitchfork and Minnie in a subdued dress.

One very memorable thing that was done for a promo event was a Mickey and Minnie in topiary costumes. It was a bit wacky. Basically there was a Mickey and Minnie topiary wandering around Epcot doing promo shots. Now that could scare your gardening-loving grandma.

Minnie is often on the merchandise for the festival and recently had the Minnie's Farmhouse Flower Shop line. This has to be towards the top in my list of favorite Flower and Garden merch. The line incorporated full color cartoon Minnie's with a very boho-chic style on different backgrounds, sometimes it was a colorful garden scene. One of the best was the apron with full color Minnie on a black and white hand drawn background of her flower shop. This scene also appeared on a few of the Dooney & Burke purse offerings. Really hoping they bring this one or something similar back.

Resorts

Value Resorts

At the All-Star Music and Sports Resorts they are building excitement for the new attraction coming to Hollywood Studios -- *Mickey & Minnie's Runaway Railroad*. Head to the food courts to check out the different artwork that adorns the walls and even the booths at All-Star Sports. The artwork features the Fab Five 5 baseball team and Minnie and her friends in different scenes.

All-Star Sports is the hotel for cheerleaders when they are there for one of the six different cheerleading competitions hosted at ESPN Wide World of Sports. The primary icon for cheerleading at Disney parks is Minnie Mouse. You can find her in plush, pins and even on shirts.

At the All Star Movies Resort in the refurbished rooms you can find a *Mickey & Minnie's Runaway Railroad* inspired art print with Mickey, Minnie and Donald.

Deluxe Resorts and Villas

You can see a statue of Minnie in her Luau gear in a display in the 1st floor of the Polynesian Resort. You will have to wander back in the depths of the Great Ceremonial House to find her. She is past the BouTiki shop and down the hallway towards Capt. Cooks. This hallway is a vintage Disney fan's dream with classic posters, island inspired Disney films and books and even a photo of Walt and his wife in a whole lot of leis.

Bay Lake Tower rooms have art prints with a pop-art style of Mickey, Goofy, and Minnie. The 1 and 2-bedroom villas have my favorite piece, a pop-art-style painting with colorful silhouettes of Mickey, Minnie and Goofy. In the 2-bedroom you get the pop art and additional artwork over the beds in the second bedroom with Minnie over one and Mickey over the other.

Mickey and Minnie have a nice quiet moment on the beach in the art print on the walls of the 1-bedroom suite at the Beach Club.

One of my favorite Minnie pieces in a hotel room at Disney is the elegant white Minnie Mouse lamp in the rooms at the Boardwalk Inn.

Minnie always has to have her signature bow! See it in the Minnie in the marble floor near the entrance of the main lobby at the Grand Floridian.

Seasonal

Minnie has the honor of hosting a meal for each season in Hollywood Studios. Get all the details in the Character Meals, Dining, and Treats section of this chapter.

Winter

For the past few years, Disney and Minnie have celebrated National Polka Dot Day on or around January 22 with a Rock the Dots event at Disney Springs. Previous events have included a special Minnie makeover at Bibbidi Bobbidi Boutique, special merchandise at over 15 shops in Disney Springs, a polka dot brunch at Paddlefish and the best part, a dance party with Minnie where she makes multiple wardrobe changes.

Spring

If you're at Disney World around Easter and looking for some eggs to hunt, head to Epcot for the Egg-Stravaganza. Minnie has been one of the eggs to find and has had the honor of being one of the eggs you can win for completing the search.

Holiday season

If you can't make it to Mickey's Very Merry Christmas Party and are looking for those festive pics, head to Animal Kingdom. It is the place with the holiday-dressed characters. You can meet Holiday Minnie and Holiday Mickey in their matching sweater and Santa hat. This is typically at their Discovery Island location, but make sure to check the app, the times guide or ask a cast member the location.

Every year Disney decorates for the holidays and the resorts are no exception. From early November to early January Disney World becomes even more magical. If you have an extra few hours and want a break from the parks head over to the Epcot resorts area. At the Yacht Club there is an incredible holiday model train set. Hidden on the backside of the train set from the main entrance of the lobby is Minnie's Christmas Candy Shop.

During the holidays pastry chefs make resort lobbies around Walt Disney World smell of gingerbread. These displays are a site to see and they smell amazing. The gingerbread house at the Grand Floridian became a holiday tradition in 1999. The primary person you will see is Santa but if you look closely above the windows there is a festive Disney touch and Minnie has been known to be on there in a wintery scene, maybe even in a sleigh with a Santa Mickey.

No Disney fan's house is complete without Mickey and Minnie holiday merchandise. For the holidays Disney releases blind pin packs, adorable plush, shirts, dinnerware and of course ornaments. There are even ornaments for many of the different resorts. The Contemporary ornament in 2018 was Mickey and Minnie with a Mary Blair inspired look. You can find the resort holiday ornaments at that resorts gift shop and often at Disney Days of Christmas in Disney Springs.

After your trip to the Disney Days of Christmas shop, pop over to the Disney Springs Tree Trail to see the Nostalgic Mickey and Minnie tree. This tree was new in 2018 and wins my award for tree with the most polka dots. The tree is bursting with decorations of three things Minnie loves: dots, bows and Mickey.

Sprinkling of Pixie Dust

Over 200. What do you think that number represents? Think, think. Merchandise? Nope. Polka dots on Minnie's red dress? Nope. It's the estimated number of different costume outfits for Minnie. Who do you think has more, Minnie or Mickey? Check out the Mickey chapter to find out!

The Magic of Minnie by Park

Minnie at the Magic Kingdom

- Minnie and Roy Disney bench, Town Square, Main Street
- Minnie PhotoPass Magic Shot, Town Square, Main Street USA
- Minnie Statue, Hub Area, Main Street USA

- Minnie in Let the Magic Begin show, Castle Forecourt Stage, Main Street USA
- Minnie in Mickey's Royal Friendship Faire, Castle Forecourt Stage, Main Street USA
- Minnie in Move It! Shake It! MousekeDance & Play It Street Party, Hub Area, Main Street USA
- Minnie in Festival of Fantasy Parade, Main Street USA, Liberty Square, Adventureland
- Meet Surprise Celebration Minnie, Town Square Theatre, Main Street USA
- Meet Halloween Minnie at Mickey's Not-So-Scary Halloween Party, special dates during the Halloween season
- Minnie in Mickey's Boo-to-You Halloween Parade, Main Street USA, Mickey's Not-So-Scary Halloween Party, special dates during the Halloween season
- Minnie in *Mickey's Christmas Carol* window display, shops on Main Street USA, during the holiday season
- Meet Holiday Minnie at Mickey's Very Merry Christmas Party, special dates during the Holiday season
- Minnie in Once Upon a Christmastime Parade, Main Street USA, special dates during the holiday season
- Minnie in Mickey's Most Merriest Celebration Stage Show, Castle Forecourt Stage, special dates during the holiday season

Minnie at Epcot

- Meet Classic Minnie, Character Spot, Future World
- Minnie Topiaries, during all 4 Epcot Festivals, usually near entrance of the park
- Minnie egg, Egg-Stravaganza, World Showcase, special dates in Spring

Minnie at Hollywood Studios

- New in 2020! Mickey and Minnie's Runaway Railway, Grauman's Chinese Theatre
- Minnie handprints, forecourt Grauman's Chinese Theatre
- Minnie in Fantasmic! nighttime show, Sunset Boulevard
- Meet seasonally dressed Minnies at Minnie's Seasonal Dine Character Meal, Hollywood and Vine
- Meet Movie Maven Minnie at Red Carpet Dream, Commissary Lane

Minnie at Animal Kingdom

- Meet Safari Style Minnie, Discovery Island
- Meet Holiday Minnie, Discovery Island, holiday season

Minnie at Disney Springs

- Minnie Rock the Dots Events, Disney Springs, January
- Minnie Dome Cake, Amorette's Patisserie
- Nostalgic Mickey & Minnie Tree, Disney Springs Tree Trail, holiday season

CHAPTER THREE

Goofy

Whether he is cutting a hole in his house to fit a giant screen TV; doing his signature Wilhelm scream; teaching us how to fish, swim or play any number of sports badly; or he is just messing with guests around Walt Disney World, you can't help but smile when Goofy is around.

Goofy has starred in more than 50 cartoons including an education film called *A Goofy Look at Valentine's Day* where Goofy learns the significance of Valentine's Day. I hope they have this on Netflix!

There is a lot of Goofy to love at Disney World and the Imagineers have a lot of fun creating stories around this character including the Great Goofini, Chef Goofy and even Santa Goofy. Goofy's friends at Disney World tend to have their work cut out for them as Goofy is –well-- Goofy and he doesn't always follow the rules. And Disney loves rules. When visiting Goofy see what mischief you can get into!

Character Meet and Greets

Meet Great Goofini, Magic Kingdom

You can't meet Pete at Pete's Silly Side Show in Fantasyland at Magic Kingdom but you can hang with the Great Goofini. At this meet and greet Goofy has traded in this signature orange shirt and green hat for a white daredevil jumpsuit. He may be the Great Goofini but it's clear Goofy is still Goofy. It seems the act might not have gone as planned and there is a crashed motorcycle in the backdrop. I'm guessing Goofy made his signature Wilhelm scream during that accident.

Tip: This attraction separates into two lines one for Donald and Goofy and one for Pluto and Daisy. Autographs: even with less than a full set of fingers Goofy does autographs. FP+: no, but the lines tend to be fairly manageable. PhotoPass photographers will be there ready to take pics with their camera or yours!

Meet Goofy, Epcot

Meet Goofy at the Character Spot in Future World at Epcot. In the past Goofy and Pluto would switch up their visits so check the app of the Times Guide guide before planning to see the Goof at this spot. He will be in his traditional garb with the vest and bright green hat. The background is a futuristic painting and at times features a monorail. Autographs: definitely. FP+: yes and recommended.

Meet Goofy, Hollywood Studios

Goofy is just hanging around on Grand Avenue at Hollywood Studios between Star Tours and the Muppets area. He's making trouble in his pretty standard Goofy get up of blue pants, orange shirt and green hat. Goofy is known for some antics and seems to have even more fun at this meet and greet. During one meet and greet with some friends he actually took off before they could take pictures and kept hitting the horn on a guests electric wheelchair. Once you can get his attention he will do autographs and pose for pics, but most days only until 4 PM. FP+: no.

Meet Dino Gaming Goofy, Animal Kingdom

Goofy is ready to go dig up some Dino Bones with his buddy Pluto at the Slam-o-Saurus in DinoLand USA at Animal Kingdom. As always, Goofy's outfits do not disappoint. He looks super spiffy in striped pants with brightly colored dinosaurs pattern, a vest covered in footprints, a boater hat and even a striped shirt with arm garters. It looks like he is going to be running some high-stakes dino poker games and the costumers outdid themselves because he looks quite spiffy. He and Pluto hang together at this meet and greet in front of a basic backdrop that has Donald's Dino Bash and a wacky looking dino on it. But really, with that costume, Goofy doesn't need any fancy backdrops. Goofy and Pluto are often around multiple times during the day until late afternoon around 5:30 PM. FP+ no

Character Meals, Dining, and Treats

Disney Jr. Play and Dine Character Meal, Hollywood Studios

Goofy is likely the tallest one in the room at the Disney Jr. Play and Dine character breakfast at Hollywood and Vine in Hollywood Studios. Goofy is on the Disney Jr. show *Roadster Racers* and is joined by his Disney Jr. friends Doc McStuffins, Vamparina, and coming in May 2019 Nancy from the show *Fancy Nancy*. Meals served: breakfast and like most character meals, it is buffet style. The same restaurant is used for lunch and dinner during Minnie's Seasonal Dine. Reservations: definitely recommend making one. These characters are very popular with the young guests. DVC Dawn tip: This meal is super fun. But know going in it's a bit crazy.

Minnie's Seasonal Dine Character Meal, Hollywood Studios

Minnie has the honor of hosting a meal for each season in Hollywood Studios and Goofy is an honored guest. All of the characters costumes change each season and there are some spiffy spring, summer, Halloween and Christmas costumes. Get the scoop on Goofy's threads at this meal in the Season section. All the details on these meals are in "Minnie: Character Meals."

Safari Character Meal, Animal Kingdom

Goofy is a character known for some shenanigans and when he is in safari gear is not an exception. Safari Donald is hosting breakfast, lunch and dinner at Tusker House in Africa in Animal Kingdom and Goofy is often on the guest list along with Mickey and Daisy. One thing that is guaranteed with Goofy is a big old hug, but at this meal Goofy has also been spotted covering kids faces in photos, reading a guests book and even doing bunny ears behind a guest head when they were taking photos.

Tusker House offers something that many character meals do not: outdoor seating. Not something most people want to do in August but maybe a nice day in January. Another thing Tusker House offers is a buffet with African Flavors. So, in addition to the standard Mickey Waffles and bacon, Tusker House has Beef Bobotie and Jungle Juice at breakfast and multiple curries and basmati rice at lunch and dinner. Not feeling adventurous? There are also Mickey Waffles or Corn Dog Nuggets, but what better place to try something new than at a buffet? With a mouse in a safari hat and a duck in khaki colored heels (referring to Daisy, not Donald.) Reservations: highly recommended.

Chef Mickey's Character Meal, Contemporary Resort

Chef's Mickey, Minnie, Donald, Goofy and Pluto are all coming out of the kitchen for photos and autographs at Chef Mickey's at the Contemporary Resort. Chef Goofy is winning all the awards in his chef hat, signature chef striped pants and chef's jacket with multiple medals. Make sure to ask Goofy to show you his medals and ask him what he won them for! Characters may vary, but these five are usually standard. You can ask when checking in which characters will be around. Meals served: breakfast, brunch and dinner. All are buffet. Reservations highly recommended. This is one of the more difficult reservations to get and this meal is very popular. If you are over at the Magic Kingdom, you can just walk to the Contemporary.

> *Tip*: though an excellent character meal and one of the rare places to have the Fab 5 together, it is also very loud and very busy.

Minnie's Beach Bash Breakfast, Beach Club Resort

Minnie, Daisy, Donald and Goofy are stopping off for a quick breakfast with you before heading to the beach. They are all dressed for a stylish day in the sand and surf with Goofy in shorts and a life jacket. This character meal is breakfast only and at Cape May Café at the Beach Club Resort. The characters have stayed fairly consistent but it's always worth asking at check in before making any promises about which of Minnie's friends will be at the beach bash. The meal is a buffet with standard breakfast options including Mickey waffles.

Tip: You can walk or take a boat into Epcot from this resort. Both options will have you entering via the International Gateway (between UK and France) in World Showcase.

Goofy's Candy Company, Disney Springs

Goofy has his own line of candy. Yep, of all the Disney characters Goofy gets a candy line. You can find the packaged candy around the parks and resorts but find the mother lode at Goofy's shop at Disney Springs. At this shop you can also get caramel apples, krispy treats and tons of other ways to sugar you up.

Goofy Dome Cake, Amorette's Patisserie, Disney Springs

Grab some friends with a sweet tooth and head to Amorette's for the Goofy Dome Cake. The cake includes chocolate chiffon, chocolate mousse, caramel mousse and milk chocolate Ganache all covering a cake that is decorated with Goofy's orange shirt, blue pants and green hat.

Rides/Attractions

Barnstormer Starring the Great Goofini, Magic Kingdom

The Barnstormer in Fantasyland at Magic Kingdom is a great first coaster for the little ones. You sit in the stunt plane of the Great Goofini who you can actually meet in Pete's Silly Sideshow. The coaster is as wacky and goofy as Goofy himself. FP+: yes and is recommended. A lot of families use this ride as the first coaster and it isn't a ride that moves through its line quickly. Height restrictions: 35"/89cm. Ride photo: no but there are a few photo spots in line and around the ride.

Tip: Looking for a less crowded route to Tomorrowland? Beyond the entrance to the Barnstormer is a somewhat secret walkway leading straight to Tomorrowland near Space Mountain. This is an excellent way to avoid the crowds on Main Street after the nighttime show. (*Theme park author Alexa*)

Mickey and Minnie's Runaway Railway, Hollywood Studios

Goofy is driving a train and for some reason, you, Mickey, Minnie and a bunch of other guests decide to get on it. That should only happen in a cartoon. Needless to say it will be a wacky ride. Thank goodness you are in a cartoon world on this all-new ride slated to open in 2020. This ride has the distinction of being the first Mickey-themed ride-through attraction. This attraction is replacing the Great Movie Ride and is inspired by the Mickey shorts that have appeared on the Disney Channel and features a new animation style. The attraction will have a new short and song created specifically for the ride.

Shows and Parades

Festival of Fantasy Parade, Magic Kingdom

Goofy is hoofing it along the parade route with his favorite chipmunks Chip and Dale in Festival of Fantasy. He is sporting quite the outfit, with a green hat, red jacket with triangle detail, blue and purple striped pants and multi-colored shoes. Make sure to check out the cool spring action on Goofy's hat. He and his get-up get the crowd pumped before the last float with Mickey and Minnie.

Mickey's Royal Friendship Faire, Cinderella Castle, Magic Kingdom

Goofy is dressed for a day in ye olde Fantasyland during this show. If you're a Goofy fan, definitely check this one out if you want to see Goofy bust out some sweet moves and a parasol. Yep, I said it. Goofy has a parasol.

Move It! Shake It! MousekeDance & Play It Street Party, Magic Kingdom

This show has the unique honor of being a parade and dance party all rolled into one. Goofy got to invite friends and family to the dance party. Goofy's son Max, Clarabelle Cow and Horace Horsecollar have all been spotted getting their groove on. Find this in the hub area by Cinderella Castle and check the app and times guide as times can vary.

Nighttime Shows

Fantasmic!, Hollywood Studios

Fantasmic! is a unique nighttime spectacular at Hollywood Studios. This jam-packed show has over 50 costumed performers who sing, dance and perform stunts on the rock formation set behind the lagoon, or on one of the many floats that glide by. There are different scenes over the course of the 30-minute show from Mickey's dreams of dancing princesses and happy elephants, to the invasion of the villains that give Mickey nightmares of snakes and dragons.

You will see over 15 Disney films projected on walls of water, cheer on Mickey as he battles a glowing dragon and snake, see fireworks and wave at over 30 live characters from a wide range of films on a boat at the end. Goofy is one of the characters on the boat waving and doing a streamer dance.

Statues, Handprints, Mini Golf, and Other Semi-Permanent Fixtures

Get a rare photo of Goofy sitting down on the Goofy bench at Magic Kingdom. This is a bronze statue of Goofy and he is quite snazzy in a purple jacket with red tie and a top hat. If you sit next to him, listen carefully as you may get an audible surprise.

Goofy is looking a bit bashful or perhaps thoughtful in his bronze statue in front of Cinderella Castle at Magic Kingdom. This is one of the few places where you can capture Goofy staying still, so it's a great place for a photo.

How many fingers does Goofy have? Find out while checking out his handprint in the forecourt of Grumman's Theatre at Hollywood Studios.

Goofy and Donald are covered in sand at the summer course at the Winter Summerland mini-golf course. Throw on your holiday Hawaiian shirt and head over to this mini-golf course. There is a winter side course and a summer side course. Goofy and Donald are proudly wielding their golf clubs for a fun sandy photo op on the summer side. The course is open most days of the year when weather permits. There are usually coupons and discounts available online or ask the concierge at your resort. Then hop on the bus towards Blizzard Beach.

Shops/Merchandise

At just about any store at Disney World you can find something Goofy. There are Goofy socks, mugs, shirts, runDisney gear, Tsum Tsums and a whole lot of excellent pins. Just check any of the main gift shops at the parks and you will find something.

Goofy is on a lot of Tower of Terror (ToT) merchandise. Make sure to visit Tower Hotel Gifts as you exit the ride in Hollywood Studios. Many of the ToT souvenirs can *only* be found in this shop. You won't find it at other shops or on the Shop Disney parks app. There is adorable Goofy plush in the ToT bellhop uniform, shirts of him on the ride and more.

Goofy makes a fun holiday ornament so make sure to check out Disney Days of Christmas at Disney Springs to see the selection. While you're at Disney Springs make sure to check out Goofy's Candy Company. This shop is chockfull of things to rot your teeth.

The souvenir shop at All-Star Sports is also called Sport Goofy and it features a number of harder- to-find sports-themed merchandise for a lot of the characters. It also has one of the best selections of Disney-themed sports balls.

One of the most popular Disney souvenirs in our house with my sons is a Disney Racer. These are cars with a design inspired by a Disney character. There's Groot, Goofy, Peter Pan and many more. They are around the parks and resorts but Test SIMporium outside of Test Track at Epcot is a good location to check.

Marathons

At the Walt Disney World Marathon, the most uncoordinated of the Fab 5 has one of the two big races! It's called Goofy's

Race and a Half Challenge and is two days of running going over 39 miles. He gets sporty at the race in his track outfit. He is often on the medal for the marathon and in 2018 he was on the medal with his pal Mickey. At the Wine & Dine Marathon Goofy sometimes hangs out in his cowboy costume.

Mickey's Parties

As part of the mouse's main gang, Goofy is at the party and ready for spooky shenanigans at Mickey's Not-So-Scary Halloween Party. Goofy gets in on the costume-wearing and hangs with Pluto and walks as part of the opening mask-wearing group in the parade.

Goofy will be at the party for a meet and greet. Like Minnie, Goofy has one of the pieces of party merchandise from 2018 I am coveting. One of the sets of pins was character with treats and Goofy has basically turned himself into a box of popcorn. His arms and legs are popping out of the box and he has popcorn on his head. Gawrsh, I love that guy.

Santa Goofy! Yep, Goofy is donning the hat and the suit for his meet and greet. This is a popular one but during the holiday season you can actually meet Santa Goofy at a few other locations so skip this one if you're tight on time. Don't skip seeing Goofy in the Once Upon a Christmastime Parade though. He is driving a huge candy bike in a great outfit with red-and-white striped pants, a green jacket and striped hat.

Clarabelle has one of the most elaborate floats and is right before Goofy's in the parade. Keep an eye out for the cookies that pop up out of the oven on the float. And make sure to take a deep inhale for a fantastic smell!

Clarabelle and Goofy also get to hang out in the Mickey's Most Merriest Celebration Stage show. Goofy is decked out for the season in an ugly Christmas sweater and pom hat. He partners with Daisy to sing a song about texting silly things during the holidays. Is this what Goofy does when he has too much eggnog? Goofy also tears it up on the fiddle.

Clarabelle is a bit more glamorous in her white gown and singing *All I Want for Christmas is You* with reindeer back up dancers. Yes. This all happens in this show.

Resorts

Value Resorts

Goofy is the goalie at the *Mighty Ducks* pool at the All-Star Movies resort. The souvenir shop at All-Star Sports is also called Sport Goofy and features one of the best selections of Disney-themed sports balls.

At the All-Star Music and Sports Resorts they are preparing guests for the new attraction coming to Hollywood Studios: Mickey and Minnie's Runaway Railroad. Head to the food courts to check out the artwork that adorns the walls and even the booths at All-Star Sports. The artwork features the Fab Five 5 as a baseball team and there's even a drawing of Goofy diving.

Goofy is once again playing sports at a pool at the All Star Sports resort. At the Homerun Hotel area the pool is shaped like a baseball diamond and Baseball Goofy is warming up the batters running the pitching gun, which actually shoots water into the pool.

> *Tip*: The All Star resorts are one of many hotels undergoing refurbishment. If you must see Goofy at any of these resorts, make sure to do a little research in advance to make sure he wasn't removed.

Need to cool off and get goofy? At the Goofy Pop Jet water play area at the Pop Century resort you can pose for a photo with Goofy and his surfboard and then get squirted by the pop jets. This area is located between the 60's and 70's sections.

Moderate Resorts

Goofy is climbing up a ladder with Mickey's nephews nearby in a display at Fulton's General Store at Port Orleans Riverside. During the holidays, the festive Goofy plush in an ugly Christmas sweater has been seen at this store. If you love Goofy or ugly Christmas sweaters this should be on your wish list.

Deluxe Resorts and Villas

Goofy is helping out his friends as part of a totem pole with Mickey, Donald and a bear at the Mercantile store in the lobby of the Wilderness Lodge.

Bay Lake Tower rooms have art prints with a pop art style of Mickey, Goofy, and Minnie. The 1 and 2-bedroom villas have my favorite piece, a pop art style painting with colorful silhouettes of Mickey, Minnie and Goofy.

Seasonal

Spring

If you're at Disney World around Easter and are looking for some eggs to hunt, head to Epcot for the Egg-Stravaganza. In the past Goofy has been one of the only eggs that you have to go inside a building to find. Maybe that's because even as an egg he can get up to no good!

From March to June Goofy is pulling out his dapper style at the Minnie's Springtime Dine at Hollywood and Vine at Hollywood Studios. Goofy is in a bright orange jacket and striped shirt with a blue vest and green pants with brown vintage-style shoes. If vintage style is your thing, definitely check out this character meal. Read all about this meal in Minnie's chapter under "Character Meals."

Summer

During the summer months Goofy throws on a pair of shorts and heads to Blizzard Beach for a meet and greet.

June to September is beach time for Goofy and his friends at Minnie's Summertime Dine at Hollywood and Vine at Hollywood Studios. Goofy is in a vest and what looks like some red Chuck Taylors.

Fall/Halloween

Halloween season at Disney starts in September and runs to early November at Minnie's Halloween Dine at Hollywood Studios. Goofy is in a spider-loving, Halloween-colors cowboy costume. He's really owning wearing color at the seasonal dine events.

Holiday Season

Right after Halloween it's time for the Holiday Dine at Hollywood Studios that runs until early January. Santa Goofy is at the meal for hugs and holiday wishes.

At Magic Kingdom grab a sweet treat and head to the windows of the Emporium to see statues from *Mickey's Christmas Carol*. Goof is Jacob Marley's ghost, scaring Scrooge in one of the windows. When you're near the Emporium shop make sure to pop in and check for Goofy on seasonal merchandise.

After Santa heads out for his all-nighter on the 24th, Santa Goofy steps in on the 25th over at Hollywood Studios. He may not say Ho Ho Ho or have a belly like a bowl full of jelly, but Santa Goofy has a red suit, a white beard, and the hat and, well, it's Goofy. Santa Goofy is usually only scheduled to be there from December 25 to December 31 so make sure he's at the top of your Christmas list.

Also at Hollywood Studios during the holiday season is the Jingle Bell Jingle Jam nighttime show. The show is on screens next to and projected onto Grauman's Chinese Theatre. The show is separated into different sections that are separated by classic holiday songs. You can see Goofy in scenes from *Mickeys' Christmas Carol* and *Hockey Homicide* during the songs "Walking in a Winter Wonderland" and "Need a Little Christmas."

Another place to meet Santa Goofy is in Animal Kingdom. Sometimes Goofy is hanging out with Pluto in his festive collar or Donald in his holiday wear. This is in DinoLand USA, but has been known to move. The background is typically dinosaur-themed but a Christmas tree helps make it a bit more festive.

Every year Disney releases a series of pins for the Christmas holiday. The 2018 set of pins were character-inspired Ugly Christmas Sweaters. Goofy was a sweater vest with a Christmas light necklace. You can find the holiday pins at Emporium shop and sometimes Ye Olde Christmas Shoppe at Magic Kingdom and Pin Trader shops around Disney World. Hey Santa Disney, can you create a shirt of this pin?

Get your holiday card photo near Disney Days of Christmas at Disney Springs. Statues of Mickey and Donald are caroling and Pluto and Goofy are decorating the tree in the festive snow covered scene.

Sprinkling of Pixie Dust

Need a bit more Goofy before heading out of your Disney bubble? Check out the fantastic Goofy statue outside the Disney Earport store at the Orlando airport. Goofy has been given the challenging task of balancing a tray piled high with Mickey Krispy treats dripping with bright pink icing. Icing is everywhere, Goofy's shoe, the floor and even the giant green hat resting behind him. This is definitely worth getting to the airport two hours before your flight.

> *Tip*: This store is before going through security, so make sure to leave a bit of extra time. This airport is known for long security lines. Also, Disney has two stores at the airport and Goofy is only hanging around with pink krispy treats at the Earport.

The Magic of Goofy by Park

Goofy at the Magic Kingdom

- Goofy Statue Bench, Town Square, Main Street USA
- Goofy Statue, Hub Area, Main Street USA
- Goofy in Mickey's Royal Friendship Faire, Castle Forecourt Stage, Main Street USA
- Goofy in Move It! Shake It! MousekeDance & Play It Street Party, Hub Area, Main Street USA
- Goofy in Festival of Fantasy Parade, Main Street USA, Liberty Square, Adventureland
- Meet the Great Goofini, Fantasyland
- Barnstormer Starring the Great Goofini roller coaster, Fantasyland
- Meet Halloween Goofy at Mickey's Not-So-Scary Halloween Party, special dates during the Halloween season

- Goofy in Mickey's Boo-to-You Halloween Parade, Main Street USA, Mickey's Not-So-Scary Halloween Party, special dates during the Halloween season
- Meet Santa Goofy at Mickey's Very Merry Christmas Party, special dates during the holiday season
- Goofy in *Mickey's Christmas Carol* window display, shops on Main Street USA, during the holiday season
- Goofy & Clarabelle in Once Upon a Christmastime Parade, Main Street USA, special dates during the holiday season
- Goofy & Clarabelle in Mickey's Most Merriest Celebration Stage Show, Castle Forecourt Stage, special dates during the holiday season

Goofy at Epcot

- Meet Classic Goofy, Character Spot, Future World
- Goofy Topiaries, during all 4 Epcot Festivals, often near entrance of the park
- Goofy eggs in Egg-Stravaganza, World Showcase, special dates in Spring

Goofy at Hollywood Studios

- Goofy in Fantasmic! Nighttime Show, Sunset Boulevard
- Coming in 2020: Goofy in Mickey and Minnie's Runaway Railway, Grauman's Chinese Theatre
- Goofy handprints, forecourt of Grauman's Chinese Theatre
- Meet Goofy, Grand Avenue
- Meet Roadster Racer Goofy, Disney Jr. Play and Dine, Hollywood and Vine
- Meet Hollywood, Springtime, Summer, Halloween and Holiday Goofy at Minnie's Seasonal Dine Character Meal, Hollywood and Vine

🐭 Meet Santa Goofy, Check the App or a Times Guide for Location, holiday season

🐭 Goofy in Jingle Bell Jingle Jam nighttime show, Grauman's Chinese Theatre, holiday season

Goofy at Animal Kingdom

🐭 Meet Dino Gaming Goofy, DinoLand USA

🐭 Meet Goofy at Safari Character Meal, Tusker House, Africa

🐭 Meet Santa Goofy, DinoLand USA, holiday season

Goofy at Disney Springs

🐭 Goofy treats, Goofy's Candy Company

🐭 Goofy sculpture in a winter scene, outside Disney Days Of Christmas

🐭 Goofy Dome Cake, Amorette's Patisserie

CHAPTER FIVE

Donald (and Daisy) Duck

Donald Duck celebrated his 50th birthday on a float in a parade with live ducks in party hats. He's appeared in over 125 cartoons, was the face of orange juice and has given millions of hugs to guests at Disney parks around the world. All while not wearing pants.

Donald will turn 85 in 2019 and it will be fun to see how Disney World chooses to celebrate. At his 50th birthday there was no Philharmagic with Donald at Magic Kingdom and no Hollywood Studios or Animal Kingdom. Cupcakes were not a big thing and instead of Instagram we had Polaroid pictures. Now real ducks at Disney World even have their own Instagram account (@ducksofwaltdisneyworld).

Character Meet and Greet

Meet Astounding Donald, Magic Kingdom

Pete's Silly Side Show in Fantasyland at Magic Kingdom features the Astounding Donald. In this circus-themed meet and greet Donald is ready for his act as a snake charmer. Donald abandons his signature blue shirt and lack of pants for a beard, fancy shirt and hat. The snake charmer at the circus photo area features the signature Disney level of detail. Want more than the standard Donald pic? This is an excellent chance to see classic characters with new personas and costumes. Donald is a talented duck and he can do an autograph. FP+: no.

> *Tip*: This attraction separates into two lines one for Donald and Goofy and one for Pluto and Daisy.

Meet Donald and maybe a few Caballeros, Epcot

Donald and a few of his Caballeros hang out outside the temple in the Mexico Pavilion at Epcot. This area can be very easy to miss. As you leave the temple and heads towards Norway, there is a small path to your left. Follow that path and at the right time Donald may be there. Check a times guide or the app to find out when. Since this is an outdoor area it can be impacted by weather and can often end earlier in the evening. Donald is wearing his mucho grande sombrero and a striped colorful poncho. FP+: Nope.

Meet Classic Donald, Hollywood Studios

Right near the entrance to Hollywood Studios is the Sid Cahuenga's One-of-a-Kind shop and it's at this shop you can get a one of a kind photo with Donald Duck. At this meet and greet Donald is usually wearing his traditional blue top with the red bowtie and blue hat. If you ask nicely, you may be able to get Donald and Daisy together. Donald is a busy duck and this is an outdoor location so he may be gone fairly early in the afternoon. Make sure to check the app or times guide. FP+: nope.

Meet Dino Loving Donald, Animal Kingdom

Donald is dressed like the mayor of his Dino Bash at his meet and greet at DinoLand USA at Animal Kingdom. Daisy went all out when designing Donald's spiffy mint green and blue texturized dino print jacket (that matches her tunic) and his panama hat with a feather Mohawk. He even has a sash covered in a print of his ancestral dinosaur.

Donald discovered his ancestors were actually dinosaurs and that's a reason to celebrate. I fully support this because any discovery that gets Daisy with a Donna Karan vibe, Goofy in arm garters and chipmunks in dino costumes is a good one. Donald is shaking hands and kissing babies across the way from the entrance to TriceraTop Spin but only until about 5:30 PM. FP+ no. Donald's Dino Bash was all-new in 2018. With the level of detail put into the costumes, storytelling and party, I am hoping it will be sticking around for a while.

Character Meals, Dining, and Treats

Safari Character Meal, Animal Kingdom

Safari Donald is hosting breakfast, lunch or dinner at Tusker House in Africa in Animal Kingdom. Mickey and Daisy don their safari gear and are usually at this character meal. Goofy has been spotted as well.

One thing Tusker House offers that many character meals do not is outdoor seating. Not something most people want to do in August but maybe a nice day in January. Another thing Tusker House offers is a buffet with African Flavors. So, in addition to the standard Mickey Waffles and bacon, Tusker House has Beef Bobotie and Jungle Juice at breakfast and multiple curries and basmati rice at lunch and dinner. Not feeling adventurous? There are also Mickey Waffles or Corn Dog Nuggets, but what better place to try something new than at a buffet? With a mouse in a safari hat and a duck in khaki colored heels (referring to Daisy, not Donald.) Reservations: highly recommended.

Minnie's Seasonal Dine Character Meal, Hollywood Studios

Minnie has the honor of hosting a meal for each season in Hollywood Studios and Donald is an honored guest. All of the characters costumes change each season and they are some spiffy spring, summer, Hollywood, Halloween and Christmas costumes. Get all the details of the meal in "Minnie's Character Meals" or just get the scoop on Donald's' threads (nope, still no pants) at these meals in "Seasonal."

Chef Mickey's Character Meal, Contemporary Resort

Chef's Mickey, Minnie, Donald, Goofy and Pluto are all coming out of the kitchen for photos and autographs at Chef Mickey's at the Contemporary Resort. Chef Donald is showing some color with a red scarf and checked apron. Characters may vary, but these five are typically standard. You can ask which characters will be around when you check in. Meals served: breakfast, brunch and dinner. All are buffet. Reservations highly recommended. This is one of the more difficult reservations to get and this meal is very popular. If you are over at the Magic Kingdom, you can just walk to the Contemporary.

> *Tip*: though this is an excellent character meal and one of the rare places to have the Fab 5 together, it is also very loud and very busy.

Minnie's Beach Bash Breakfast Character Meal, Beach Club Resort

Minnie, Daisy, Donald and Goofy are stopping off for a quick breakfast with you before heading to the beach. They are all dressed for a stylish day in the sand and surf with Donald in his brightly colored beach shirt. This character meal is breakfast only and is offered at Cape May Café at the Beach Club Resort. The characters have stayed fairly consistent but it's always worth asking at check in before making any promises about which of Minnie's friends will be at the beach bash. The meal is a buffet with standard breakfast options including Mickey waffles.

Donald's Dino Bash Cupcake, Animal Kingdom

Head to Restaurantosaurus in DinoLand USA to try the Donald's Dino Bash Cupcake. It is not quite as cute as Chip and Dale in dinosaur costumes but it's fairly close. It's a yellow cake topped with blue frosting and then a swirl of white frosting. It's topped with a red bow and yellow crunchies. This may only be available for a limited time but Disney doesn't usually have a bash or party without some sort of special treat.

Rides/Attractions

Mickey's Philharmagic, Magic Kingdom

The attraction in Fantasyland at Magic Kingdom may be called Mickey's Philharmagic but Donald is the star. This is a 3D movie, a chance to sit in comfy seats in air conditioning and be entranced by some Disney magic featuring many favorite characters.

At the end of the show, Donald is shot out of a tuba straight into the back wall. With a bit of magic and some animatronics

Donald legs are sticking out of the wall when the lights come up. When my youngest was 5 we saw the show multiple times because he loved this part.

Seeing Donald hanging with Jasmine, Simba and some of your favorite Disney characters is a must for any Donald fan. FP+: offered but not usually necessary. No height restrictions or ride photo but there is a great photo op with a Donald statue in the shop at the exit of the show.

Jungle Cruise, Magic Kingdom

Hidden in the Jungle Cruise in Adventureland at Magic Kingdom is a Donald Duck! AP Jamie learned about this hidden Donald on a behind-the-scenes tour she did a few years ago. Find Donald hanging in the jungle in the area where the native's boats are on the sandy shore. Take a look at the middle boat and get a load of that beak! It's your favorite duck Donald!

Gran Fiesta Tour, Epcot

The Gran Fiesta Tour Starring the Three Caballeros in the Mexico Pavilion at Epcot is a gentle boat ride through various scenes in Mexico. There is also live action footage of Mexico with the Three Caballeros added in. My favorite is seeing Donald rock diving with the professionals towards the end of the ride. Can you help Panchito and José find all the Donald's during the ride? Pay close attention to that piñata the children are giving a whack. Height restrictions: no. FP+: no. Ride Photo: no but there are many *maravilloso* photo ops around the Mayan temple. PhotoPass Photographers have been spotted at the top of the winding staircase that leads down into the marketplace area.

> *Tip*: San Angel Inn is the main restaurant inside the building. Head over there and put in your name for a delicious meal on the waterfront. While you're waiting for your table, hop on the boat ride to help work up your appetite.

Shows, Parades & Dance Parties

Festival of Fantasy Parade, Magic Kingdom

Donald and Daisy are rocking the polka dots on their *Fantasia*-inspired float in the Festival of Fantasy Parade. Donald even has on a polka dot hat and bowtie. I think this may top my list of favorite Donald outfits.

Mickey's Royal Friendship Faire, Cinderella Castle, Magic Kingdom

Do you think Donald can dance? Yeah, he can. He and Daisy both get their groove on and even jump in this show. Not sure I've ever seen a duck jump before, especially not whilst wearing a puffy Shakespearean style hat. Donald then changes up his costume when hanging with the gang from the Snuggly Duckling gang from the movie *Tangled*. For this scene Donald has some fur and a Viking helmet. It's a look.

Move It! Shake It! MousekeDance & Play It Street Party, Magic Kingdom

This show has the unique honor of being a parade and dance party rolled into one. Donald is shaking his tail feathers with some Cabelleros friends. Get the time on the app or from a cast member then head toward the hub in front of Cinderella Castle.

Donald's Dino Bash & Dino-riffic Dance Party, Animal Kingdom

Donald's Dino Bash is a place to see characters and have a Dino-Riffic Dance Party. The prehistoric fun is in DinoLand USA at Animal Kingdom. All the fun takes place right near the entrance to Primeval Whirl. The highlight is the Chipmunk-O-Saurus, which is Chip and Dale in colorful dinosaur costumes. Honestly, it's one of the cutest costumes on a character I've seen.

It's a dance party and they are there to show off their pre-historic moves so posed pictures and autographs are not likely to happen but all three have meet and greet locations before the dance party. Now this whole event was new in 2018. It seems fairly popular so hopefully has staying power as Animal Kingdom doesn't have too many characters shows or a parade.

Nighttime Shows

Fantasmic!, Hollywood Studios

Fantasmic! is a unique nighttime spectacular at Hollywood Studios. This jam-packed show has over 50 costumed performers who sing, dance and perform stunts on the rock formation set or on one of the many floats that glide by.

You will see over 15 Disney films projected on walls of water, cheer on Mickey as he battles a glowing dragon, see fireworks and wave at over 30 live characters from a wide range of films on a boat at the end. Donald is one of the characters on the boat waving and doing a streamer dance.

Statues, Mini Golf, Handprints and Other Semi-Permanent Fixtures

Donald is one of the most animated of the bronze statues in the hub area in front of Cinderella Castle at Magic Kingdom. He is wearing his signature hat and sailor inspired top.

Donald made a visit to Grauman's Theatre in Hollywood Studios and left some wing prints for you to find.

Goofy and Donald are covered in sand at the summer course at the Winter Summerland mini-golf course. Throw on your Hawaiian shirt and head over to this mini-golf course. There is a winter side and summer side and Goofy and Donald are proudly wielding their golf clubs for a fun sandy photo op. The course is open most days of the year when weather permits. There are usually coupons and discounts available online or ask the concierge at your resort. Then hop on the bus to Blizzard Beach.

Games

Each time you visit the Firehouse on Main Street USA to play Sorcerers of the Magic Kingdom you receive a new pack of cards. There are over 70 different cards including Caballero Donald's Piñata. There are special cards during Mickey's Not-So-Scary Halloween Party and Mickey's Very Merry Christmas Party like the Huey, Dewey and Louie Snowfort Barricade.

Shops/Merchandise

Are you curious what happened to Donald after his musical mishaps in the Mickey's PhilharMagic attraction? Visit Fantasy Faire in Magic Kingdom to find out. It's just outside Mickey's PhilharMagic and has a huge sculpture of Donald with the angry horn section behind him. There's always some Donald merchandise to be had in this area.

Have a little duckling? There are some sweet baby clothes at Emporium at Magic Kingdom, Disney Studio Store at Hollywood Studios, and Discovery Trading Company at Animal Kingdom. You can also stock up on Donald supplies for the kitchen at Mickey's Pantry in Disney Springs.

Donald has a whole store named after him at All-Star Movies - Donald's Double Feature. You can find a number of angry and happy Donald mugs, shirts and pins at this shop.

The DisneyStyle store at Disney Springs opened in 2018. This is the place to go for fun, quirky merchandise. Donald has some perfect hoodies, tunics and shirts at the shop if you're looking to DisneyBound this famous duck. The line features the classic Donald blue color that his fans love to see him in.

Marathons

At the Walt Disney World Marathon Donald hosts one of the runs and gets sporty in a coach outfit. He is often on a medal for the marathon and in 2018 he was on it with his pal Mickey. You might see Knight Donald cheering you on at the Disney Princess Marathon. At the Wine & Dine Marathon Donald has been spotted in his Chef uniform and in a Frontier Donald outfit.

> *Tip*: Wear that medal loud and proud around the parks! You earned those congratulations on the days after your race! This is a great opportunity for some fun pictures, conversations with other guests and cast members, and it just feels great! (Disney podcaster/marathoner Mike)

Mickey's Parties

As one of Mickey's favorite ducks, Donald is always on the guest list and in his costume for the Mickey's Not-So-Scary Halloween Party. Donald has been a regal knight and a surprisingly cute Jack-o-lantern. He is typically on the float with Mickey, Minnie and Daisy in the parade and can usually be found for a meet and greet with Daisy.

Donald comes out again at Christmas time. At Mickey's Very Merry Christmas party, DVC Dawn was able to get pictures with Scrooge and Donald together. Now that is rare. Donald is often dressed as a lumberjack for the meet and greet. He has a black and red checked earflap hat and shirt.

Donald changes it up for the parade, though, with a red jacket that compliments Daisy's red dress.

Speaking of Daisy, in Mickey's Most Merriest Celebration stage show Donald responds to Daisy's text and shows up to the party with his cell phone and a kind of hipster holiday get-up. He has a hat, a green check vest and red shirt. Also during this show Donald's Caballeros buddies show up for some holiday tunes *en Español* including Feliz Navidad.

Epcot Festivals

During Festival of the Arts at Epcot the characters have paintings near their typical meet and greet areas. Donald's meet and greet area is tucked into a garden area to the Norway side of the Mexico pavilion. Unlike his princess friends Donald has done a self-portrait and even signed it. He is *muy festivo* in his portrait with a sombrero and serape and of course he is *sin pantalones*.

Donald's topiary is a staple at Flower & Garden Festival. Where he is, what exactly he is doing, and who he is with tends to change. In 2018 he was hanging with his nephews Huey, Dewey, and Louie near the backside of Spaceship Earth. Another year he was holding a trowel with his nephews in a colorful garden of yellow flowers. He will definitely be there, so grab your festival passport and map and do a little search.

Donald's friends the Caballeros also have a topiary at Flower & Garden that is usually near the Mexico Pavilion.

They are vibrant and have great props. They all have their hats and one of them even has a bowtie.

If you want to get friendly with a character notorious for annoying Donald, check out the Spike's Pollen Nation Exploration. Spike is a cute innocent-looking bee that loved to terrorize Donald in movies in the 1940's and 50's. Spike's Pollen Nation is a scavenger hunter for flower lovers of all ages.

To play you pay around $6-10 to purchase a map and set of stickers. Then hunt around the festival for the Spike statues hidden in the gardens around World Showcase. Keep track of where you have found Spike with your sheet of stickers. Once you've buzzed around and found them all take your map to a redemption station to get a prize. The prizes tend to change each year and in 2018 there were 4 different sets of patches to choose from: Mickey, Minnie, Figment or just general flower and garden ones. This is a playful way to explore the festival and learn about some flowers...and who doesn't love stickers and patches?

Resorts

Value Resorts

Head to the All-Star Music Resort and take a dip in the guitar-shaped calypso pool. While there get squirted by Donald and the Caballeros. At All-Star Sports on the giant tennis courts in the Center Court area is a statue of Donald showing his angry side as he is trying to play tennis. Statues of his nephews Huey, Dewey and Louie are on the other side of the net but are playing baseball instead.

At the All-Star Movies Resort there is a small statue of Donald and Daisy from *Fantasia 2000*. It's a bit random and tricky to find. Just head behind the Sorcerer Mickey pool and the two are in a landscaped area outside of the pool area. In the refurbished rooms you can find a *Mickey & Minnie's Runaway Railroad* inspired art print with Mickey, Minnie and Donald in the room.

Moderate Resorts

Coronado Springs Resort has a Spanish Colonial Mexico vibe and is in my top five resorts at Disney World. It's undergoing a huge refurbishment that started in 2017 and will continue until an all-new tower is open. The new resort is a bit less colorful than before but the grounds are still beautiful, the food options are excellent and the new rooms feel more deluxe than moderate.

I stayed at Coronado in the middle of construction in spring of 2018 and loved it. To apologize for the construction our room came with a rare set of "Under Construction" Three Caballeros pins. All three are in Mickey hard hats and are ready to work with a paintbrush, saw and construction sign. In the newly refurbished rooms there are multiple art prints of the Three Caballeros. If you are looking for Donald and the Caballeros goodies to bring home, the shop Panchito's is the place to go. When in this shop, make sure to look towards the ceiling to find some Three Caballeros paintings on the brickwork.

Every now and then a character makes a little visit to a resort pool. If it's going to happen, it will usually be when there is entertainment at the pool. Cast members run different games throughout the daytime at the bigger pools at the resorts. Donald has been spotted helping out with the games at the Caribbean Beach Resort.

Donald is being driven crazy by nephews Huey, Dewey and Louie and Chip at Fulton's General Store at Port Orleans Riverside Resort. This is probably one of the most elaborate displays at a resort shop in Disney World.

Deluxe Resorts and Villas

Donald has his own splash pad at Saratoga Springs Resort. Over near the High Rocks Springs pool a happy looking Donald is holding a bucket and ready to escape the Florida heat.

In the 1 and 2-bedroom Beach Club Villas your ducklings can snooze with Donald in a themed trundle bed. This new style of beds is popping up around many Disney resorts, making it a bit easier to squeeze five people in one hotel room. Rather than just have a blank piece of wood or board when the trundle bed is opened, Disney worked their magic and there is a painting of Donald snoozing on the beach.

Donald is in a totem pole with his friends Goofy, Mickey and a bear at the Mercantile store in the lobby of Wilderness Lodge.

Donald and a few of the other Fab Five are cleverly part of the design in the marble floor near the entrance of the main lobby at the Grand Floridian.

Seasonal

Spring

If you're at Disney World around Easter and looking for some eggs to hunt, head to Epcot for the Egg-Stravaganza. Donald must love Easter because he is looking quite happy in his egg form. He has been in the group of character eggs that you have to find.

From March to June Donald is pulling out his dapper kind-of-Scottish style at the Minnie's Springtime Dine at Hollywood and Vine at Hollywood Studios. Donald has a purple blazer with red vest and red and purple checked hat. If vintage style is your thing, definitely check out this Character Meal. You can also eat how cartoon ducks eat with a buffet section called Donald's Delectable Entrees. Read all about this meal in "Minnie's Character Meals."

Summer

June to September is beach time and Donald is on lifeguard duty at Minnie's Summertime Dine at Hollywood and Vine at Hollywood Studios. He even has a lifeguard whistle.

Fall/Halloween

Halloween season at Disney starts in September and runs to early November at Minnie's Halloween Dine at Hollywood Studios. Donald is ready for trick or treat in a space costume that feels a bit Buzz Lightyear with white and lime green details.

Holiday Season

Right after Halloween it's time for the Holiday Dine at Hollywood Studios, which runs until early January. Donald is actually in the most colorful costume with a holiday green and red vest with a matching plaid hat. Donald definitely likes wearing plaid at these meals.

See Donald as a snowman and battling his nephews Huey, Dewey and Louie in the Jingle Bell Jingle Jam nighttime show at Hollywood Studios. The show is on screens next to and projected onto Grauman's Chinese Theatre. The show is separated into different sections that are separated by classic holiday songs. You can see Donald in scenes from *Mickeys' Christmas Carol* and *Donald's Snow Fight* during the songs *Jingle Bells* and *Need a Little Christmas*.

Donald tends to be a popular character for holiday merchandise. He was seen building a snowman with his nephews on a set of holiday pins in 2018. He also had one of the collectible ugly-holiday sweater pins available in blind packs that year and was on some dinnerware helping Mickey and Goofy carry a Christmas tree. Head to the Disney Days of Christmas at Disney Springs or the Emporium shop at Magic Kingdom to find a lot of the holiday goodies. While at Emporium check out the window decorations with Donald, Mickey and Scrooge in scenes from *Mickey's Christmas Carol*.

A Santa Donald statue has been spotted hanging out at the Zawadi Marketplace at Animal Kingdom Lodge around Christmastime. The display does not look permanent so it's probably worth asking before making a special trip. It's common to see Mickey and Goofy as Santa, but not as many Donalds.

Get your holiday card photo near Disney Days of Christmas at Disney Springs. Statues of Mickey and Donald caroling while Pluto and Goofy are decorating the tree in the festive snow-covered scene.

Sprinkling of Pixie Dust

A World of Magic: Donald goes global! Many Disney characters are in the parks in other countries in a variety of ways, including treats. The Donald desserts at Tokyo Disneyland and DisneySea are some of the most fun Disney has had with a Donald dessert. Maybe its' not a park you can visit anytime soon, but it's definitely worth a quick search online.

The parks in Japan have had a few fun Donald-themed treats including a bun that looks like Donald is in a raft. My personal favorite is the Donald Duck Butt Dessert. Seriously, that is the name of the dessert. And no, in case you're wondering, he is not wearing pants in this dessert!

The Magic of Donald by Park

Donald at the Magic Kingdom

- Donald Statue, Hub Area, Main Street USA
- Get a Donald card, Sorcerer's of the Magic Kingdom, Main Street USA
- Donald in Mickey's Royal Friendship Faire, Castle Forecourt Stage, Main Street USA
- Donald in Move It! Shake It! MousekeDance & Play It Street Party, Hub Area, Main Street USA
- Donald in Festival of Fantasy Parade, Main Street USA, Liberty Square, Adventureland
- Meet the Astounding Donald, Fantasyland
- Donald in Mickey's Philharmagic attraction, Fantasyland
- Donald Statue in Fantasy Fair shop, Fantasyland
- Meet Halloween Donald at Mickey's Not-So-Scary Halloween Party, special dates during the Halloween season
- Donald in Mickey's Boo-to-You Halloween Parade, Main Street USA, Mickey's Not-So-Scary Halloween Party, special dates during the Halloween season
- Meet Festive Donald at Mickey's Very Merry Christmas Party, special dates during the holiday season
- Donald in *Mickey's Christmas Carol* window display, shops on Main Street USA, during the holiday season
- Donald in Once Upon a Christmastime Parade, Main Street USA, special dates during the holiday season

🐭 Donald in Mickey's Most Merriest Celebration Stage Show, Castle Forecourt Stage, special dates during the holiday season

Donald at Epcot

🐭 Meet Donald and maybe a few caballeros, Mexico

🐭 Grand Fiesta Tour ride, Mexico

🐭 Donald Topiary, during all 4 Epcot Festivals, often near entrance of the park

🐭 Donald Painting, Epcot Festival of the Arts, Mexico

🐭 Donald egg in Egg-Stravaganza, World Showcase, special dates in Spring

🐭 Play Spike's Pollen Nation scavenger hunt, Epcot Flower and Garden Festival

Donald at Hollywood Studios

🐭 Meet Classic Donald, Sid's Porch, Hollywood Boulevard

🐭 Donald in Fantasmic! nighttime show, Sunset Boulevard

🐭 Donald wing prints, forecourt, Grauman's Chinese Theatre

🐭 Meet Hollywood, Springtime, Summer, Halloween and Holiday Donald at Minnie's Seasonal Dine Character Meal, Hollywood and Vine

🐭 Donald with his nephews in Jingle Bell Jingle Jam nighttime show, Grauman's Chinese Theatre, during the holiday season

Donald at Animal Kingdom

🐭 Meet Dino Loving Donald, DinoLand USA

🐭 Donald's Dino Bash & Dino-Riffic Dance Party, DinoLand USA

🐭 Donald's Dino Bash Cupcake, DinoLand USA, Limited Time Only

Meet Donald at Safari Character Meal, Tusker House, Africa

Donald at Disney Springs

 Donald sculpture in a winter scene, outside Disney Days of Christmas

DAISY DUCK

Daisy isn't officially part of the Fab 5 but is often found in similar locations and since she puts up with Donald and his antics she has earned a spot in this section. Daisy and Minnie Mouse are also good friends and can often be found together. They share a mutual love of bows and fabulous heels, which are almost always part of their costumes.

Character Meet and Greets

Meet Madame Daisy, Magic Kingdom

Madame Daisy Fortuna is ready for fortune telling at Pete's Silly Side Show in Fantasyland at Magic Kingdom. Daisy has one of the most elaborate costumes in the group with multiple headscarves, an ornate vest and some fancy white bloomer looking pants. And you can't forget Daisy's signature heels, this time in a bright lime green. The space is themed to look like the back of Daisy's packed traveling show, complete with a suitcases, a birdcage and even a water can. FP+: no but the lines tend to be fairly manageable. PhotoPass photographers will be there ready to take pics with their camera or yours!

Tip: this attraction separates into two lines one for Donald and Goofy and one for Pluto and Daisy. If you have the time definitely visit all four for some of the greatest show photos. Like Donald, Daisy has duck talents and can give autographs.

Meet Daisy, Epcot

If you want to start your day at Epcot with a bit of Daisy, head towards your right as soon as you reach Spaceship Earth. Look for the duck in the perky pink dress, purple bow and pink heels.

Disney may decide to mix it up and have other characters in this space and it's not usually all day. Often it is in the morning only. Next time instead of rushing to Soarin or Frozen Ever After stop at this spot for a hug, autograph and photo. Daisy and Pluto have been known to switch around. Daisy heads back to the Friendship Ambassador Gazebo near the entrance to World Showcase while Pluto pops up and greets guests at Legacy Plaza West. FP+: no.

Meet Classic Daisy, Hollywood Studios

Right near the entrance to Hollywood Studios is the Sid Cahuenga's One-of-a-Kind shop and it's at this shop you can get a one of a kind photo with Daisy Duck. At this meet and greet Daisy is usually wearing her traditional pink dress, pink heels and purple bow. If you ask nicely, you may be able to get Donald and Daisy together. Daisy is a busy duck and this is an outdoor location so she's typically gone fairly early in the afternoon. Make sure to check the app or times guide. FP+: nope.

Meet Designer Daisy, Animal Kingdom

Donald was having a party and needed someone to create all the party gear so he turned to Daisy. Check out all Daisy's fantastic design skills when you meet her at her Design Studio in DinoLand USA. She has set up her inspiration board with fabrics and drawings of the character costumes off the Cretaceous Trail. She even has a dinosaur friend with a coral-colored scarf to match his skin tone.

This is a Daisy must-visit just to see her amazing costume and to see the design board, which she loves to show off. Daisy is looking straight fashion designer diva with a purple headscarf, fantastic sunglasses atop her head, a colorful shawl and lime green shoes. But the best part is the tunic, which is mint and light blue and has a texturized dinosaur skin print. Daisy and her costume team have outdone themselves with these prehistoric looks. Daisy has many fashionable parties in the evening so she is done meeting her fans around 5:30 p.m. FP+ no.

Character Meals, Dining, and Treats

Minnie's Seasonal Dine, Hollywood Studios

Minnie has the honor of hosting a meal for each season in Hollywood Studios and Daisy is a fellow bow-wearing guest. All of the characters costumes change each season and they are some spiffy spring, summer, Hollywood, Halloween and Christmas costumes. Get all the details of the meal in "Minnie's Character Meals" or just get the scoop on Daisy's dresses and lovely shoes at these meals in "Seasonal."

Safari Character Meal, Animal Kingdom

Daisy is pulling on her khaki heels to join Donald and Mickey for breakfast, lunch or dinner at Tusker House in Africa in Animal Kingdom. Goofy has been spotted at this character meal also. Daisy is wearing a safari inspired dress, hat and of course those heels. Like most character meals, Tusker House is pretty busy, big and can be fairly loud.

Unlike most character meals, Tusker House has outdoor seating and a buffet with African Flavors. So in addition to the standard Mickey Waffles or corn dog nuggets, Tusker House has Beef Bobotie and Jungle Juice at breakfast and multiple curries and basmati rice at lunch and dinner. Buffets are the perfect place to be adventurous and try something new. Reservations: highly recommended.

Minnie's Beach Bash Breakfast, Beach Club Resort

Minnie, Daisy, Donald and Goofy are stopping off for a quick breakfast with you before heading to the beach. They are all dressed for a stylish day in the sand and surf with Daisy in a tropical blue dress, a striped headband with a bow and pink heels. This character meal is breakfast only and at Cape May Café at the Beach Club Resort. The characters have stayed fairly consistent but it's always worth asking at check in prior to making any promises about which of Minnie's friends will be at the beach bash. The meal is a buffet with standard breakfast options including Mickey waffles.

Main Street Confectionery, Magic Kingdom

Next time you are on Main Street, take your time to look in the windows. They are typically decorated with characters. Daisy has been known to be one of the decorations in the windows at Main Street Confectionery.

Shows and Parades

Festival of Fantasy Parade, Magic Kingdom

Daisy is channeling her inner clown with Donald on their *Fantasia* inspired float in the Festival of Fantasy Parade. Daisy is mixing her stripes and dots with a pink and green dress and a bow that is half pink and green stripes and half green and purple polka dots. It's quite a look but Daisy is pulling it off and is tying it all together with purple heels with a yellow bow.

Mickey's Royal Friendship Faire, Cinderella Castle, Magic Kingdom

Ducks can dance. I had no idea. Donald and Daisy totally show their mad duck moves in this show. Most of the costumes have a Shakespearean/Elizabethan vibe and Daisy is even donning a garland. I know what you're thinking... Is she wearing heels? Heck yeah. Daisy keeps up with all of Donald's moves and she does it in purple heels.

Shops/Merchandise

Daisy is one of those characters you can find on merchandise but she is often with her friend Minnie. Always check the main souvenir shops if you're having a hard time finding her. If that search doesn't get you the shirt or mug you're craving, ask a cast member. She is a very well-loved character.

With her new role as fashion designer behind Donald's Dino Bash you can find Daisy merchandise at Chester and Hester's Dinosaur Treasures at Animal Kingdom. Look for plush, shirts, toys and more at the shop.

Do you love taking selfies at Disney? So do Daisy and Minnie. They even have a pin of them doing a selfie in front of the castle. Find it at most pin shops at the parks and resorts.

The Tsum Tsum craze from Japan has hit the US. Some people say it's already starting fade here but Daisy makes a really cute little stuffed creature. She has been in a number of the series seen in the parks or that are even inspired by the parks. Tsums can be tricky to find but Stage 1 Company Store at Hollywood Studios and Once Upon a Toy at Disney Springs are shops to check.

Mickey's Parties

Mickey knows that one of the ways to a woman's heart is through her friends so Daisy is always on Mickey's party guest list. Daisy has a beautiful blue princess costume she wears to meet and greet and while on a float with a few of the Fab 5 in the Boo to You Parade at Mickey's Not-So-Scary Halloween Party.

Daisy knows how to pull together a festive outfit! At Mickey's Very Merry Christmas party she wears a bright red dress with snowflake detail and matching bow. It's picture perfect. One year AP Jamie and her boyfriend DisneyBounded as holiday Donald and Daisy. "I just wore a red cardigan with snowflake stickers that matched Daisy's dress and a sparkly red skirt. When I went to see Daisy she knew immediately and was so excited. Everyone DisneyBounds Mickey, Minnie and princesses. We try and do a character that doesn't get quite as much attention and they just love it. Daisy was so excited she even pulled Minnie over to show her my ensemble and bow!"

During the party, Daisy and Minnie do a meet and greet together and both are dressed in their holiday best. Daisy has a different fancy holiday outfit to match Donald for the Once Upon a Christmastime Parade. Daisy has quite the holiday ward- robe as she is also in the Mickey's Most Merriest Celebration stage show as well. In this show she is super high-tech and is texting with Donald. Daisy and some of her friends then do a song and dance about texting at the holidays. It's...interesting.

Epcot Festivals

Daisy is one of the most colorful topiaries at the Flower & Garden Festival with her bright pink eye shadow and bow covered in little flowers. She tends to change locations every year so grab that passport and map so you can check her off your list.

Seasonal

Spring

If you're at Disney World around Easter and looking for some eggs to hunt, head to Epcot for the Egg-Stravaganza. Even as an egg Daisy looks happy. She has been on the list of eggs to find during your hunt.

From March to June, Daisy is on the dress and guest list at the Minnie's Springtime Dine at Hollywood and Vine at Hollywood Studios. Daisy is competing with Mickey and his pink blazer for my favorite outfit with her floral dress with a green shiny sash, fancy flowered bow and the best part, mint colored heels. If vintage style is your thing, definitely check out this character meal. Read all about this meal in "Minnie's Character Meals" section.

Summer

In June – September Daisy is ready to hit the beach at Minnie's Summertime Dine at Hollywood and Vine at Hollywood Studios. Ducks must dress up for the beach, because Daisy is in yellow heels and a fabulous summer hat that go perfectly with her floral beach cover up.

Fall/Halloween

Halloween season at Disney starts in September and runs to early November at Minnie's Halloween Dine at Hollywood Studios. Daisy is with Minnie on the spider theme with an orange and purple dress and a Halloween purple bow

Holiday Season

Right after Halloween it's time for the Holiday Dine at Hollywood Studios that runs until early January. Daisy is ringing in the season with a green tunic with sparkly snow-flakes along the lace edging. The best is her festive red heels with a matching green bow.

The Magic of Daisy by Park

Daisy at the Magic Kingdom

- 🐭 Daisy in Mickey's Royal Friendship Faire, Castle Forecourt Stage, Main Street USA

- 🐭 Daisy in Festival of Fantasy Parade, Main Street USA, Liberty Square, Adventureland

- 🐭 Meet Madame Daisy Fortuna, Fantasyland

- 🐭 Main Street Confectionery Window, Main Street USA, this changes regularly so may be different when you are there

- 🐭 Meet Halloween Daisy at Mickey's Not-So-Scary Halloween Party, special dates during the Halloween season

- 🐭 Daisy in Mickey's Boo-to-You Halloween Parade, Main Street USA, Mickey's Not-So-Scary Halloween Party, special dates during the Halloween season

- 🐭 Meet Holiday Daisy with Holiday Minnie at Mickey's Very Merry Christmas Party, special dates during the holiday season

- 🐭 Daisy in Once Upon a Christmastime Parade, Main Street USA, special dates during the holiday season

- 🐭 Daisy in Mickey's Most Merriest Celebration Stage Show, Castle Forecourt Stage, special dates during the holiday season

Daisy at Epcot

- 🐭 Meet Daisy near Spaceship Earth or toward the entrance to World Showcase at the Friendship Ambassador Gazebo

- 🐭 Daisy Topiary, during most Epcot festivals, usually near entrance of the park

- 🐭 Daisy egg in Egg-Stravaganza, World Showcase, special dates in Spring

Daisy at Hollywood Studios

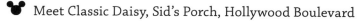 Meet Classic Daisy, Sid's Porch, Hollywood Boulevard

Meet Hollywood, Springtime, Summer, Halloween and Holiday Daisy at Minnie's Seasonal Dine, Hollywood and Vine Restaurant

Daisy at Animal Kingdom

Meet Designer Daisy, DinoLand USA

CHAPTER SIX

Pluto

You know when you're out walking and you see a dog and they're just so happy to see you? They're wagging their tail and wiggling their butt and are so excited you're there and it just makes you smile? That is what it's like interacting with Pluto at Disney World. Except Pluto walks around on two legs not all fours.

Pluto is incredibly high-energy, friendly, and just loves to dance and play with guests. This pup has been in over 50 cartoons and has been through a lot. He was harassed multiple times, even at Christmas, by Chip 'n' Dale, gets pushed around at his own birthday by Mickey's nephews and is even abducted by aliens.

Pluto, like the other members of the Fab 5, is a staple at Disney World. You will see him pretty regularly on everything from meet and greets to merchandise. Where he really shines is in parades where he shows off some very plucky dance moves.

Character Meet and Greets

Meet Wonder-Pup Pluto, Magic Kingdom

Pete's Silly Side Show in Fantasyland at Magic Kingdom features Wonder-Pup Pluto. In this circus-themed meet and greet Pluto is ready for his act with a tower of pink poodles as his backdrop. This was previously Minnie's space but it has been updated to have far less pink and more red and blue props. Pluto is wearing a red ringmaster hat and a special collar.

Pluto is quite the talented pup. In addition to training other dogs he can also sign autographs. FP+: no.

Tip: this attraction separates into two lines one for Donald and Goofy and one for Pluto and Daisy. Wonder-Pup Pluto moved to this space during the 2019 celebration for Mickey and Minnie's birthday. The celebration is slated to end in fall 2019. It will be interesting to see if Pluto stays or moves back up to his previous spot up near Town Square and Magnifique Minnie returns to Pete's Silly Side Show.

Meet Pluto, Epcot

Pluto goes global at his meet and greet in World Showcase. He is at the Friendship Ambassador Gazebo that's right near the entrance to World Showcase. The gazebo is decorated with posters from some of Pluto's favorite countries. It is right after you cross the bridge from Future World heading towards World Showcase. If you hit Mexico or Canada you've gone too far. Pluto is wearing a very colorful collar with a special nametag. FP+ no. Visit early or during lunch as the area closes well before the park, usually before sundown, and can have long lines.

Tip: Daisy and Pluto are known to switch places with Pluto hanging out up near Spaceship Earth at Legacy Plaza. Check the app or ask a cast member where you can find your favorite pup.

Meet Dino Fan Pluto, Animal Kingdom

Pluto and his spiffy Dino-loving pal Goofy are ready to go dig up some bones at the Slam-o-Saurus in DinoLand USA at Animal Kingdom. Pluto is sporting a fossil-covered bandana and a bone-shaped tag with his name on it. The two are in front of a basic backdrop that has Donald's Dino Bash and a wacky looking dino on it. But really, with Goofy's costume and the fun the two of them have together, basic is good. Goofy and Pluto are typically around multiple times during the day until late afternoon around 5:30 PM. FP+ no.

Tip: During the holiday season Pluto and Goofy change up their costumes and add a few festive touches to this meet and greet.

Character Meals, Dining, and Treats

Chip 'n' Dale's Harvest Feast Character Meal, Epcot

Chip 'n' Dale and Pluto are getting along at the character meal at the Garden Grill Restaurant in the Land Pavilion. Pluto is a frequent visitor but is not always a given at this family-style all-you-can-eat restaurant for breakfast, lunch and dinner. If Pluto is a must, make sure to call Disney dining to see if Mickey's best friend is on the schedule.

Even if Pluto is not there, there are so many cool things about this restaurant, including the fact that it spins so you can see different parts of the Living with the Land attraction while you are dining. And your favorite pal Mickey is there in his farmer gear. Oh and your vegetables at dinner are grown in that attraction. Reservations: highly recommended. Arrive early and ask to sit on the lower level to get one of the booths.

Chef Mickey's Character Meal, Contemporary Resort

Chef's Mickey, Minnie, Donald, Goofy and Pluto are all coming out of the kitchen for photos and autographs at Chef Mickey's at the Contemporary Resort. Chef Pluto has a diner vibe going on, with a full-length white apron and floppy hat. Make sure you get Pluto to show you his special tag that he wears just for this event. Characters may vary, but these five are typically standard. You can ask when checking in which characters will be around. Meals served: breakfast, brunch and dinner. All are buffet. Reservations highly recommended. This is one of the more difficult reservations to get and this meal is very popular. If you are over at the Magic Kingdom, you can just walk to the Contemporary.

> *Tip*: though this is an excellent character meal and one of the rare places to have the Fab 5 together, it is also very loud and very busy.

Shows and Parades

Let the Magic Begin, Magic Kingdom

Let the Magic Begin is a 5-minute stage show with multiple characters there to welcome you to a magical day at the park. It happens most days before Magic Kingdom opens. Pluto is bringing all his puppy energy to the show.

Festival of Fantasy Parade, Magic Kingdom

Pluto is joining Donald and Daisy on their *Fantasia* inspired float in the Festival of Fantasy Parade. Pluto even has a special jester-looking collar and fancy tag for the event.

Move It! Shake It! MousekeDance & Play It Street Party, Magic Kingdom

This show has the unique honor of being a parade and dance party all rolled into one. Pluto is known for his dance moves and does not disappoint at this dance party that typically happens a few times a day in the hub area in front of Cinderella Castle.

Nighttime Shows

Fantasmic!, Hollywood Studios

Fantasmic! is a unique nighttime spectacular at Hollywood Studios in a stadium that was specifically designed just for it. This jam-packed show has over 50 costumed performers who sing, dance and perform stunts on the rock formation set or on one of the many floats that glide by. There are different scenes over the course of the 30-minute show from Mickey's dreams of dancing princesses and happy elephants, to the invasion of the villains that give Mickey nightmares of snakes and dragons.

You will see over 15 Disney films projected on walls of water, cheer on Mickey as he battles a glowing dragon and snake, see fireworks and wave at over 30 live characters from a wide range of films on a boat at the end. Pluto is one of the characters on the boat waving and doing a streamer dance.

Statues, Mini Golf, and Other Semi-Permanent Fixtures

Pluto is one of a few characters with small bronze statues around the hub in front of Cinderella Castle at Magic Kingdom. Pluto looks as happy as always with his tongue hanging out and one paw in the air.

Pluto is playing in the snow over at the Winter Summerland mini-golf course. Put on your Disney ugly Christmas gear and head over to this mini-golf course. There are winter and summer side courses. Pluto is over on the winter side hanging out with Minnie and Mickey near the Merry Moguls hole. The course is open most days of the year when weather permits. There are usually coupons and discounts available online or ask the concierge at your resort. Then hop on the bus towards Blizzard Beach.

Shops/Merchandise

People love to cuddle with a pup and there is Pluto plush everywhere at Disney World. If you love *Pluto's Christmas Tree*, look for the Pluto with Chip n Dale pin. He looks annoyed the same way he does in the film.

There are also not-so-cuddly Pluto souvenirs. Fine art prints and collectible figurines are available at Art of Disney in Epcot. See Pluto in a whole new way in the figurine series by Britto. The figurines remind me a lot of *Coco*, when Dante the dog is transformed into his colorful glowing spirit guide (or *alebrijes*) form. These figurines were seen floating around Panchito's at Coronado Springs and Art of Disney in Epcot and Disney Springs.

Eat your Pluto with Amorette's Patisseries at Disney Springs Pluto Dome cake.

One of my favorite Pluto souvenirs is Pluto moonlighting as the dog from Pirates of Caribbean. It's just like the ride and film except instead of the brown dog it's Pluto looking innocent with the keys to the jail hanging from his mouth. Check Plaza del Sol Caribe in Adventureland at Magic Kingdom.

Marathons and PhotoPass Magic

One of the races during the Walt Disney World marathon is the Walt Disney World 5k, which is a family friendly race. Pluto is often a friendly face at the race ready to cheer you on. He is usually on the medal for this race.

Pluto has a bit of PhotoPass magic to add to your Disney pictures. There are no guarantees on these, as Disney likes to mix it up in the photo department, but if there is a particular movie, character or photo you are looking for, ask a PhotoPass photographer and they are happy to help or direct you where to go. At Hollywood Studios in front of the arch outside Star Wars Launch Bay I've had a magic video with Mickey in a top hat and cane strolling and whistling while Pluto pops in and sits in a chair.

Mickey's Annual Parties

Pluto is on the invite list at both the Halloween and the Christmas party. At the Halloween party he appears in the parade and does meet and greets with a whimsical almost handmade-looking lions mane. At the Christmas party Pluto usually has on his snowflake Santa hat and has a shiny snowflake tag attached to his bright red collar.

At Mickey's Very Merry Christmas Party Pluto once again leads off the parade. Pluto is so high energy. He must have some espresso in his puppy chow. He and a group of characters with their holiday scarves lead off the Once Upon a Christmastime Parade. Pluto also helps his friends have a jolly holiday in the Mickey's Most Merriest Celebration stage show.

Epcot Festivals

Pluto's topiary at the Flower and Garden Festival tends to move around and be a bit different every year. He is often right up in the front of the park in front of Spaceship Earth with Mickey and Minnie. He's been seen holding a string of sausages from a picnic basket and wearing a flowery collar. Pluto may also be in topiaries during other festivals.

Resorts

Value Resorts

Your little pups can cuddle up with Pluto at the Pop Century resort. In the rooms with a pull-down bed, the artwork once the bed is open is a pop-art style painting of Pluto snoozing in front of his dog bowl. When it's not time for sleeping, that bed becomes a table.

Moderate Resorts

Lounge on the beach with Pluto and Mickey on the fold-down bed at Caribbean Beach Resort. When the bed folds-down there is a sweet painting that your little beach goer can enjoy before bed.

Deluxe and Villa Resorts

Near the entrance of the main lobby at the Grand Floridian Resort there is a marble floor with a few characters cleverly woven into the design. See if you can spot Mickey's best friend Pluto.

Seasonal

If you're at Disney World around Easter and looking for some eggs to hunt, head to Epcot for the Egg-Stravaganza. Pluto is one of the eggs in the hunt. If you were a Pluto egg at Epcot where would you hide?

In 2017 Pluto became famous for his ugly Christmas sweater. For the holiday season there was a Pluto in a green Christmas sweater and Santa hat popcorn bucket. The bucket became one of the most sought-after souvenirs during that season so it will be interesting to see it if comes back or what will top it in future years.

Chip 'n' Dale are having a little holiday fun with their pal Pluto at the Jingle Bell Jingle Jam nighttime show. See it during the Holiday season, usually early November to early January at Hollywood Studios. The show is on screens next to, and projected onto Grauman's Chinese Theatre. The show is separated into different sections that are separated by classic holiday songs. You can see scenes from *Pluto's Christmas Tree* during the songs "Jingle Bells" and "Need a Little Christmas."

Pluto has on his Christmas dog collar and is ready to help pull Santa Goofy's sleigh in DinoLand USA at Animal Kingdom. With the Donald's Dino-Bash some holiday meet and greet locations may change. In the past merry Pluto and Santa Goofy hung out in DinoLand USA with a tree covered in dinosaur ornaments.

Every year Disney decorates for the holidays and the resorts are no exception. From early November to early January Disney World becomes even more magical. If you have an extra few hours and want a break from the parks head over to the Epcot resorts area. At the Yacht Club there is an incredible holiday model train set. Hidden on the backside of the train set from the main entrance of the lobby is Mickey's Village and Pluto has come to visit.

During the holidays pastry chefs make resort lobbies around Walt Disney World smell of gingerbread. These displays are a sight to see and smell amazing. The gingerbread house at the Grand Floridian has been a holiday tradition since 1999. The primary person you will see is Santa but if you look closely above the windows there is a festive Disney touch and Pluto has been known to be on there in a wintery scene.

Pluto also appears on some of the new holiday merchandise that is released every year. Mickey is always on holiday goods and is often with either Minnie or Pluto. If you're looking for Christmas present ideas for your pup, go to the Disney Springs Tree Trail and check out the Pluto tree. The tree is covered in Disney chew toys and even has a leash garland. It's award? Best Tree for gift ideas for your dog.

Grab a festive holiday treat of poutine or a sweet cake from Amorette's Patisserie then head towards the Disney Days of Christmas at Disney Springs to check out the holiday windows and then take a pic in a winter scene with Mickey, Donald, Goofy and Pluto.

The Magic of Pluto by Park

Pluto at the Magic Kingdom

- Meet Wonder-Pup Pluto, Pete's Silly Side Show, Fantasyland
- Pluto Statue, Hub Area, Main Street USA
- Pluto in Let the Magic Begin show, Castle Forecourt Stage, Main Street USA
- Pluto in Move It! Shake It! MousekeDance & Play It Street Party, Hub Area, Main Street USA
- Pluto in Festival of Fantasy Parade, Main Street USA, Liberty Square, Adventureland
- Meet Halloween Pluto at Mickey's Not-So-Scary Halloween Party, special dates during the Halloween season
- Pluto in Mickey's Boo-to-You Halloween Parade, Main Street USA, Mickey's Not-So-Scary Halloween Party, special dates during the Halloween season
- *Mickey's Christmas Carol* windows, shops on Main Street USA, during the holiday season
- Meet Festive Pluto at Mickey's Very Merry Christmas Party, special dates during the holiday season
- Pluto in Once Upon a Christmastime Parade, Main Street USA, special dates during the holiday season
- Pluto in Mickey's Most Merriest Celebration Stage Show, Castle Forecourt Stage, special dates during holiday season

Pluto at Epcot

- Meet Pluto, Friendship Ambassador Gazebo, entrance to World Showcase or in the Legacy Plaza area
- Meet Pluto, Chip 'n' Dale's Harvest Feast Character Meal, Future World West

- Pluto Topiary, during all 4 Epcot Festivals, often near entrance of the park
- Pluto egg in Egg-Stravaganza, World Showcase, special dates in Spring

Pluto at Hollywood Studios

- Pluto in Fantasmic! nighttime show, Sunset Boulevard
- Pluto PhotoPass Magic, Animation Courtyard
- Pluto in Jingle Bell Jingle Jam nighttime show, Grauman's Chinese Theatre, holiday season

Pluto at Animal Kingdom

- Meet Dino-Loving Pluto, DinoLand USA
- Meet Holiday Pluto, DinoLand USA, holiday season

Pluto at Disney Springs

- Pluto sculpture in a winter scene, outside Disney Days of Christmas
- Pluto Dome Cake, Amorette's Patisserie
- Pluto Tree, Disney Springs Tree Trail, holiday season

APPENDIX A

How to Use This Guide: Extended Version

Welcome to the extended version of how to use this guide! This section is structured to match what you will find in the movie and characters chapters, and is the place for details on the many different ways to experience these movies and characters at Walt Disney World -- details like the time of parades, descriptions of all the different marathons, past special events, information to help you plan your trip and tips. A trip to Disney World always requires tips. And, there are a lot of tips sprinkled throughout.

Character Meet and Greets

You know, the typical give 'em a hug and have them sign an autograph book. In the past, and at other Disney Parks outside Walt Disney World, characters used to wander around. It was always so magical to be walking along World Showcase at Epcot and suddenly Pinocchio, Mickey and Donald are there.

These days most character meet and greets have designated areas and lines. For some you can even get a FastPass+ (FP+). It's less spontaneous but the positive is you can find them on the app and there's almost always a PhotoPass photographer willing to grab your mobile and snap a few pics. Unless I specifically mention it is NOT possible, the character will give their autograph and a PhotoPass photographer will likely be there.

> *Tip*: I've seen people ask characters to sign T-shirts and pillowcases. Just make sure you're not wearing

it. Characters aren't allowed to sign anything while it's on your body. *(Disney blogger Serena)*

If you love meeting characters, you can thank Disney fans in the 1950's. As theme park author Alexa explains, "the reason Disney Parks have characters to meet in the first place is because, before Disneyland even opened, fans would write to Walt Disney asking if they could meet Snow White and Mickey Mouse. Now anybody can meet them at any Disney Park!"

Characters Meals, Dining and Treats

More hugging, but this time with Mickey waffles or mac and cheese. This section includes character meals, of course, but also character-free dining that will immerse you in the story. There are also treats inspired by your favorite character or movie. Disney is all about the treats. These can be sweet or salty and in some cases are available only for a limited time. Menus, especially in the sweet treats category, tend to change regularly.

You'll always be able to find a Mickey ice cream bar or apple but for the rest there is no guarantee. In this section I'll give you some examples of great treats and where to find them but with the disclaimer that the menu when you're in the magic may be a bit different.

Rides/Attractions

This is where you will find the magical experiences that typically include roller coasters, 4D movies or swirling saucers.

Shows, Parades and Dance Parties

Magic Kingdom is really the park with the most parades and stage shows. All three other parks have had parades in the past but at the time of publication, it's all Magic Kingdom (unless you consider Stormtroopers marching through Hollywood a parade.) The seasonal parades and shows are in the Mickey's Parties or Seasonal section.

Festival of Fantasy Parade, Magic Kingdom

Festival of Fantasy is the afternoon parade that takes place on most days at Magic Kingdom. The parade usually starts in Frontierland and winds it way through Liberty Square then down Main Street. Like most Disney parades there are characters, intricately detailed floats, characters, Disney-esque choreography performed by cast members in magnificent costumes, music and more characters.

If you want an amazing backdrop for your photos, watch the parade from the end of Main Street as close as possible to Town Square. For smaller crowds, head over to Frontierland or Liberty Square. The parade is about 12 minutes long. Festival of Fantasy has been around since 2014 so it may only be a matter of time before we see something new march into Magic Kingdom.

FP+: not at the time of publication, but there is a Festival of Fantasy Dining Package where you get to stand in a space reserved for a smaller crowd.

Tip: During the Holiday season there may be other parades. The week of Christmas through New Years, Mickey's Once Upon A Christmastime Parade runs, and may replace Festival of Fantasy. You may also see special parades and shows that are being recorded for Disney television specials.

Mickey's Royal Friendship Faire, Magic Kingdom

Mickey's Royal Friendship Faire is a 22-minute stage show at the Magic Kingdom on the Cinderella Castle Forecourt Stage, the stage in front of the castle. This show is chock full of characters from princesses and princes to the Fab 5. There's dancing, singing, a few fireworks and some neat costumes for the characters you won't see anywhere else.

This show happens 4-5 times a day, depending on the weather. Hear music and see characters from *Princess and the Frog*, *Tangled*, and *Frozen*. Anywhere in the hub will give you a good view. During early fall, usually around September, there is a change in the final song for fall and another change in November for the Christmas holiday.

Move it! Shake it! MousekeDance It!
Street Party, Magic Kingdom

This parade was new in 2019 as part of the celebration of Mickey and Minnie's 90th birthday. This Street Party is all about showing off your moves. You'll be wandering around the hub in front of the castle and all of sudden a catchy tune starts and floats start appearing. That means it's time for a dance party.

This show is a parade/dance party where the floats travel down Main Street and then stop, circling the hub in front of Cinderella Castle. All of the characters are dressed in party clothes and some of them jump off their floats and come and dance in the crowd.

The character list includes Mickey, Minnie, Donald and Daisy, Goofy, Pluto and a few rare characters including Goofy's son Max, Clarabelle Cow, Horace Horsecollar, Clarice the Chipmunk, and even the Caballeros. Some characters tend to come out and dance in the crowd. They won't usually stop for autographs but time it right and you can get a photo. Typically, Donald, Goofy, Mickey and Minnie stay on their floats while some other characters may wander out into the crowd.

The party usually happens a few times a day for about 20-25 minutes. The music is catchy, and around the end of the year includes a few holiday songs. There's a hashtag Disney asks you to tag your photos and they may show it on their twitter feed or on a float that randomly rides around the park after the party. The best place to see everything is to be right smack in front of Cinderella Castle. Make sure to move around and see all the different characters though. This is not like a typical parade where you can't move an inch for fear of losing your viewing space.

Let the Magic Begin, Magic Kingdom

There was a time when Magic Kingdom did an opening show just outside the main entrance in front of the train station. Then there would be a rope drop and the rush down Main Street to beat the lines for popular rides like Space Mountain and Seven Dwarfs Mine Train. At the time of publication that show is now moved inside the park to the stage in front of Cinderella Castle and is called Let the Magic Begin.

The 5-minute show features multiple characters including Mickey Mouse. The best viewing spot is in front of Cinderella Castle. This show only happens once a day and is about 5 minutes before the park opens to the public. The times may change if there is a special event or Mickey's party, so check the My Disney Experience app or ask a cast member.

If you're already up early, see the show. It's sweet, quick and with a simple storyline that even the littlest of kids or Dug in your group can make it through without getting bored. There are princesses, a prince, Pluto and even a few evil stepsisters. It's quite the mix of characters and they are really able to show off their personalities. My understanding is that the characters may change so the only promise to make on who will be seen is Mickey and a princess.

Nighttime Shows and Dessert Parties

There are more than you might think! Each park now has at least one and often several nighttime shows. It's an opportunity to see your favorite movie projected on a castle, or a tower or even a tree! If crowds aren't your thing, check out this area for information on Dessert Parties. Yes, the parties include desserts but they also have reserved seating or standing for the nighttime shows. If you've ever crammed yourself into the hub at Magic Kingdom for fireworks, you know why reserved seating may be a worthwhile vacation investment. The seasonal nighttime shows are in the Mickey's Parties or Seasonal section.

Happily Ever After, Magic Kingdom

Disney is known for its enchanting nighttime shows and Happily Ever After at Magic Kingdom is no exception. This show is a stunning combination of fireworks, projections on the castle, music and memorable moments, quotes and all new animations from Disney and Pixar movies. Disney Imagineers have really outdone themselves with the powerful storytelling and as Executive Creative Director Michael Jung says, "paint the sky with fireworks" that are perfectly timed to dance along with the music and clips. Happily Ever After happens most evenings at the Magic Kingdom, sometimes twice. Mickey's Halloween and Christmas parties and the weather may impact show time.

The show is about 20 minutes long and has eight scenes. The story begins with a powerful quote and the melodic all new song "Happily Ever After." The show continues with Dreams featuring Tiana, Ariel, Remy, Rapunzel, and Quasimodo; Journey with Merida, and characters from Pixar favorites *Bug's Life*, *Cars*, *Finding Nemo*, and *UP*, as well as *Moana*; next is Friendship with *Aladdin*, *Tarzan*, *Lion King*, *Toy Story*, *Jungle Book*, *Wreck-it Ralph*, *Big Hero 6*, *Zootopia*, *Inside Out*, and *Monsters Inc.* After Friendship there is Love with Olaf, *Wall-E*, *Lion King*, *Tarzan*, *Zootopia*, *Finding Dory*, *UP*, and *Dumbo*; then the show goes a bit deeper and shows some villains with Adversity showing famous battles from *Mulan*, *The Incredibles*, *Little Mermaid*, *Lion King*, *Aladdin*, and *Sleeping Beauty*.

The last scene is Triumph featuring Mufasa from *Lion King*, music from *Hercules*, and each of the characters in the show having their triumphant moment. Then the castle turns gold with stained glass windows of the characters in the show. The finale begins with a moving challenge from the narrator and the show ends with Tinker Bell sprinkling some magic over the crowd and a dazzling array of fireworks. Phew! It's a jam-packed emotional 20 minutes.

There are a lot of places to stand for this show but try and make sure you are in the hub with a direct line of sight to the castle. The Fireworks Dessert Party will guarantee an excellent view. If you don't want to fork over those dollars, try standing in the hub grass area in front of Crystal Palace. Just like a Broadway show, standing close or far away will give you a different experience but neither is bad, you'll just pick up different details.

I prefer farther back to get the whole picture as the effects are not just on the castle but also the structures to the sides of the castle. The narration and original score combined with the songs we all know from movies gives me the chills every time. Regardless of which movie or character is your favorite, make the time to see this show.

Fantasmic!, Hollywood Studios

The excitement of Fantasmic! starts as you weave your way down a long road to reach the theater. It's a surprisingly long walk! Along the way there are vendors selling light up swords and Sorcerer Mickey's with spinny arms. Inside, all of the seating is built around a giant lagoon. During the show you will see over 50 costumed performers sing, dance and perform stunts on the rock formation set or on one of the many floats that glide by during the show.

One piece that is truly dazzling is the projections onto giant walls of spraying water. You'll see scenes from over 15 movies including *Lion King, Sleeping Beauty, Jungle Book, Mulan*, and even *Lady and the Tramp*. This show is also jam-packed with characters from Maleficent as a dragon to Lilo and Stitch doing a streamer dance.

There are different scenes over the course of the 30-minute show from Mickey's dreams of dancing princesses and happy elephants to the invasion of the villains that give Mickey nightmares of snakes and dragons. The snake and dragon battles can bit intense. My son Oliver saw it when he was five and did get a bit scared. He was so glad he stuck it out and I strongly encourage you to take any scared folks for a short walk around the theater if it gets to be too much. Make sure to head back to your seats as soon as the dragon is gone because you won't want to miss the end.

Toward the end is one of my favorite moments in the show! This is when a boat appears that is piloted by a black-and-white Steamboat Willie. The boat is bursting with over 30 colorful characters. The characters move around the boat waving streamers so you will likely get to see each one. It's amazing to see the contrast of the black-and white-boat with Steamboat Willie with the colorful costumes of Mulan, the Seven Dwarfs, and Rafiki.

Oliver's favorite part of the show is when Mickey defeats the dragon and appears on the top of the mountain triumphant. Oliver even stood up, raised his arms and yelled, "Go Mickey!"

Fantasmic! is an enchanting blend of storytelling, effects, clips and music from films and a massive amount of characters. And speaking of that water, be careful. In the first few rows you may get wet.

Fantasmic! has a FP+. I would recommend saving that for Toy Story Land and other shows and do the Fantasmic! Dining Package. With a dining package you reserve a meal at a pre-selected restaurant and a space at the Fantasmic! show. You have to show up for the meal and order from a specific Fantasmic! Dining Package menu.

Once you get to Fantasmic!, there is reserved seating specifically for the dining package. This theater is huge but it can fill up. The Dining Package is available with meals at Mama Melrose, Hollywood Brown Derby or Hollywood & Vine. Why not make it a character-palooza day and do the Disney Jr. Play n Dine or the Minnie's Seasonal Dine at Hollywood and Vine? The cost is based on location.

There is also a Fantasmic! Dessert package but it's pricey and just includes dessert and special seating. For not that much more you can get a full meal and maybe even see Goofy dressed as Santa!

Disney Movie Magic, Hollywood Studios

In 2017 Hollywood Studios introduced a new nighttime show honoring many of the Disney live action movies. The show is projected onto Grauman's Chinese Theatre and a series of screens to the left and right of the theatre.

The show is a spectacular celebration of Disney movies from *Mary Poppins* to *Guardians of the Galaxy*. The show opens with audio and video of Walt Disney sharing a few of his famous quotes. It's a moving tribute to Walt and is one of those moments that may give you the tingles. Towards the end there is a quote from the movie *Saving Mr. Banks*, starring Tom Hanks as Walt Disney.

Fingers crossed with the new Wonderful World of Animation show coming in May of 2019 and the opening of Star Wars Land this show will have some staying power and will remain in the rotation of nighttime shows at Hollywood Studios.

Tip: Hollywood Studios is home to multiple nighttime shows: Disney Movie Magic, Fantasmic!, Star Wars Spectacular and a few seasonal shows. Make sure you check the app or times guide to make sure they are showing the one that's on your must-see list. Once you get into the movies/character section of this book, the seasonal shows info is under Seasonal. Star Wars Spectacular is covered in Star Wars.

More Nighttime Magic coming soon...

At the D23 Destination D event at Walt Disney World in November 2018 Disney announced new nighttime shows for both Hollywood Studios and Epcot.

Joining the nighttime lineup in May 2019 is The Wonderful World of Animation a nighttime spectacular at Hollywood Studios. This will be a projection show on the Chinese Theatre, like Disney Movie Magic. During the show Mickey will take guests on a journey through 90 years of animation.

Moments from *Sleeping Beauty*, *The Incredibles*, *Coco*, and many more have been in the list shared by Disney. With 90 years of animation covered, the show will hopefully include your Disney favorite.

In 2019 at Epcot, the nighttime show Illuminations Reflections of Earth will be replaced by a temporary show called Epcot Forever. At the time of publication the timing provided for the temporary show was Fall 2019. This name and timing may change. It's not clear whether this will include any Disney movies or characters.

What Disney fans are really excited about is the all-new Epcot show coming in 2020 that Disney has said will be "a celebration of how Disney music inspires guest from all over the world." The new show will have fireworks, obviously, but concept art also show characters from *Moana*, *Pocahontas*, *Aladdin*, *Mulan*, and of course, *Frozen*. You can't have a show about Disney music without a little tune from Arendelle. The Disney Parks blog is a good source to keep up with the latest news on this show.

Tree of Life Awakenings, Animal Kingdom

Tree of Like Awakenings is a projection show at Animal Kingdom that is not as well known as the other shows. Maybe that's because there is no booming announcement when it starts. It's one of those shows you just happen upon and are so glad you did because it's mesmerizing.

Tree of Life Awakenings has four different five-minute shows that happen every 10 minutes starting at dusk. The most popular of these being the Disney Medley, which features music and pro-jections inspired by some of the best Disney animal films.

This is one of those Disney shows that is difficult to describe because the magic is so incredible. Imagineers use lighting effects to make it appear as if the animals carved into the tree are moving, and the branches look as if they are shimmering and blowing in the wind. Like other nighttime shows, it utilizes projections, this time onto the base of the tree to tell different stories. In the Disney Medley you will hear music and see animals inspired by from *Tarzan*, *Jungle Book*, *Lion King*, and *Pocahontas*. There are also animals inspired by *Bambi*, *DINOSAUR*, and *Finding Nemo*.

Most people are leaving the park and just happen to catch bits of the show. I suggest you make sure to see it. The best viewing spot is right in front of the tree on Discovery Island with the exit to the park behind you.

Rivers of Light, Animal Kingdom

Rivers of Light is another nighttime show at Animal Kingdom but is not detailed in this book as it is not a Disney movie or character driven story. That means if you're looking for The Jungle Book or Lion King you will be disappointed. It's a visually stunning show with a strong story but this is its primary mention, as this guide is all about the movie-driven experiences.

Statues, Fountains, Mini-Golf and Other Semi-Permanent fixtures.

Some characters get a whole village in a land, others have adorable statues in the hub. There are some amazing pictures to be had at these locations. You'll notice that this section will change names in the movie and character chapters as it is based on what the semi-permanent fixture actually is.

This section focuses on what you can find in the parks but if you need even more, check the resorts section. There are even more statues, larger-than-life sculptures and even movie-themed pools!

Did you know Disney World has two themed mini-golf courses? With four parks, two water parks, Disney Springs and regular special events I have honestly never stepped foot on a mini-golf course at WDW but they are included here in case you want to putt-putt. The courses are themed and some statues of movies and characters can be found at them.

Games

Gaming at Disney World takes on a few different forms. There are in park interactive games, scavenger hunts and now VR experiences at Disney Springs. In some games, characters play a big role, so it's a great way to engage with rare characters from dragons to Stormtroopers. I'm providing some general information on the games here. If you want to know if you can see your favorite movie or character check out Games in their chapter.

Magic Kingdom

Sorcerers of the Magic Kingdom is an interactive game you can play throughout the Magic Kingdom. It features over 95 minutes of original animation with Disney classic characters and villains.

Upon signing up to play at the Firehouse on Main Street USA each player receives a pack of cards featuring a lot of favorite Disney and Pixar characters. Some guest really love collecting the cards and finding rare characters like the Country Bears, Bolt, Robin Hood and Governor Ratcliffe. There are special cards during Mickey's Not-So-Scary Halloween Party and Mickey's Very Merry Christmas Party.

A Pirate's Adventure – Treasures of the Seven Seas in Adventureland. Like Sorcerers of the Magic Kingdom, this is an interactive game involving cards that will take you on a treasure hunt around Adventureland. There are five missions that will take about 30 minutes to complete. The cool part is that there is no time limit to complete them. Complete all five missions and you get a special prize. The game closes about 30 minutes before Adventureland closes.

Epcot

This park is definitely the place to visit if you love scavenger hunts. Agent P's World Showcase Adventure is usually available-year round and is one of my family's favorite games to play at Disney World (this may change to a *Duck Tales*-themed game).

All four Epcot festivals have some sort of scavenger hunt featuring a character. Find them in the Epcot Festivals section.

Animal Kingdom

Do you want to be like Russell from UP? Then you should do the Wilderness Explorers program at Animal Kingdom. You can earn your badges just like Russell. This is more of an exploration than a game. It will have you learning about animals from troop leaders, playing drums, talking to cast members from Asia about their country and even deciphering secret code words. There are over 30 different activities.

Explorers use the provided stickers and special handbook to track completion. The program is free and it may take multiple trips so make sure to hang onto your handbook because once you complete all the activities and earn all the badges, there is a special prize.

Disney Springs

If Virtual Reality is more your gaming style, hop a bus or boat to Disney Springs. When there, visit the The Void , which is in the Marketplace area. The VR experiences at the time of publications are Star Wars Secrets of the Empire and Ralph Breaks VR, inspired by the movie *Ralph Breaks the Internet*. Costs may vary so check the website for details. Since this is at Disney Springs, theme park admission is not required.

Resorts

Most resorts have an arcade. It can be a nice way to burn some time on a non-park day or on your travel day. Make sure to check out the pinball machines in the resort arcades. You may be able to play with some of your favorite movies or characters like Star Wars or Pirates of the Caribbean.

Shops/Merchandise

This is the section where you will find suggestions on the best shops to find merchandise. There are also a few examples of fun items seen at Disney World in the past on everything from dresses to mugs.

Each park has 1-2 main shops that are just huge and have a lot of merchandise. At Magic Kingdom it's Emporium on Main Street and Big Top Souvenirs in Fantasyland. Epcot has Mouse Gears, Hollywood Studios has a row of shops on both Hollywood and Sunset Boulevards; and Animal Kingdom is home to Island Mercantile and Discovery Trading Company. All the resorts have a gift shop and most have a few items themed to their resort or that are specific to it such as ornaments, shirts and pins.

Disney Springs is an excellent place to visit if you are looking to shop or get photos. Make sure to visit the Disney Co-op Marketplace for multiple concept shops with merchandise not easily found elsewhere.

New in 2018 was the DisneyStyle shop with quirky fashions, accessories, office supplies, plush and ears. There are also quirky photo spots to go along with your new souvenirs. The dressing rooms exterior walls have artwork inspired by it's a small world, churros and Mickey pretzels are on the table displays and there's a wall of Minnie ears for each day of the week. There is even a chair made from a retired teacup from the ride.

When at Disney Springs most people end up at the world's largest Disney character store, World of Disney. This giant store had a huge refurbishment in 2018. The newly laid out store has different themed-sections including those for Disney Princesses and Star Wars. There are also small homages to Disney animation. Check out the posters behind the cash registers. There are also large projection walls in a few places in the store that serve as both photo backdrops and an easy visual cue for the merchandise that can be found.

Merchandise at Disney World is constantly changing so everything in this section comes with the disclaimer of "Disney changes stuff. A lot." If the exact item I shared is not available any longer, keep looking because there is likely something in the same shop or nearby. Cast members are also an excellent source of insider information on where to find items. Just like us, they all have their favorites.

Tip: the Shop Disney Parks app is every shoppers dream. If you're looking for merchandise for a specific movie or character go into the app and start a search. Then you will see a list of search options. Pick character and then choose from that list. If you're looking for something obscure say Hercules, go into the Disney Movies section and a whole list of options will pop up. The app will then show the stores at Disney World where the item is available. If it's available for purchase on the app you can also get a little Disney magic shipped directly to you.

Special Events, Tours, Marathons, and PhotoPass Photos

There are marathons, Incredible or Frozen Summers, and other magical events that Disney holds throughout the year. There are also a number of tours of parks and resorts that can take you behind the scenes. All of these typically include some sort of magical PhotoPass Photo opp.

This category is fairly all encompassing of all the things that didn't nicely fit in the other categories. Special events especially vary greatly and often change annually. With the upcoming 50th anniversary expect a major party. My only hope is that they don't turn the castle into a big pink cake as it was for the 25th. Seriously. That happened.

Special Events

For the past few years there have been special events when movies are released or new attractions are coming. Most summers Disney tends to go all out for a summer blockbuster or a new attraction they are promoting. Some of the events are even worth facing the stifling heat of summer in Orlando to see.

In 2018 it was an Incredible Summer. Party goers got super at Glow Dance Parties, munched on Edna Mode No Capes Just Crepes sundaes and got a PhotoPass Magic Shot with Jack Jack shooting lasers from his eyes. Similar events have taken place in the past for Frozen with special parades, treats and even the Frozen Summer Games with Olaf and Sven at Blizzard Beach.

For 2019 Magic Kingdom is host to the Mickey & Minnie's

Surprise Celebration As with most Disney special events there is merchandise and specialty food and beverages. Minnie and Mickey have special party costumes that you can see when you visit them at their new meet and greet together at Town Square Theatre.

Also during the summer months of 2019 is the Glow Dance Party at Typhoon Lagoon, a whole lot of Pixar with Cars, Incredibles, and Monsters Inc. special events at Hollywood Studios and a Lion King dance party at Animal Kingdom. But the one I am most excited about is the return of the Guardians of the Galaxy Awesome Mix live at Epcot. As the mom of a die-hard Marvel fan, anything superhero is a win. Star Wars fans are also getting a special treat in late summer of 2019 with the opening of part of the all-new highly anticipated Star Wars Galaxy's Edge at Hollywood Studios. My husband and son are both excited for this one.

runDisney Marathons

Running is magical, for some folks, and Disney has become quite the host for marathon runners with four different marathons. Disney marathons are not like any other marathon. Where else will Mickey and Minnie cheer you over the finish line? Or Dopey is on your medal? Or you go off course to hang with Darth Vader?

At these events, there are character meet and greets and cool backdrops themed to the race. Characters are also on the medals! The medals do tend to change every year.

- Walt Disney World Marathon, typically in January. The characters at the event and on the medals tend to be fairly consistent.

- Disney Princess Half Marathon, usually in mid to late February where Disney Podcaster Mike may be too sweaty to hang with the Princesses, but has seen fellow runners get engaged with the help of some Disney royalty. Each year this marathon changes up its theme. One year it was Frozen, another Beauty and the Beast. This tends to change up the princesses, their friends at the event a little and changes the medals a lot. (I would love if that scene in Ralph Breaks the Internet with Vanellope and all the princesses were the inspiration for a race. You could get pics with all the princesses in their pajamas and Cinderella would have a glass slipper she could break on a chair in her race photo.)

- Star Wars themed marathon, often in April. "This is an amazing opportunity for any Star Wars fan to run with the force!" Disney Podcaster Mike. The characters at the event, and on the medals, tend to be fairly consistent.

- Disney Wine & Dine Marathon in November. "The best part about this race is that you are at Walt Disney World during the Food & Wine Festival, and while Mickey's Not-So-Scary Halloween Party is going on! It's a great time to be at Walt Disney World and the races are the icing on the cake!" – Disney Podcaster & Marathoner Mike. For this race a character or characters host each run and the medals tend to feature that host. This is an excellent race if you love World Showcase, food and food-loving Disney characters like Chef Louie and Sebastian from *Little Mermaid*.

At each race there are characters there to cheer you on, sign autographs and take pictures. You may be sweaty but so is everyone else so just go for it. This is a chance to see some rare characters. Past events have been visited by Soccer Player Minnie, the Mice from Cinderella, Cruella De Vil and Jack Sparrow.

> *Tip*: Make sure you have Memory Maker; the race pictures are included. You are going to get some amazing shots of you in action and with characters. You will always want to have these memories to share with friends, family, and of course, to show off on social media! (Disney podcaster/marathoner Mike)

Go for the ultimate challenge, like the Dopey challenge, which is 48.6 miles in one weekend to receive special medals. "The Dopey Challenge is the ultimate experience for any Disney runner! It's four mornings of magic with others that are just as crazy as you are! There is huge camaraderie with the other Dopey Challenge participants, and you are pushing yourself to the limit by Sunday. You are there for every mile, every smile, and every moment of Marathon Weekend," shares 4-time Dopey challenge runner Mike.

Is your preferred location at a marathon on the sidelines? No worries. Disney gets that and has packages and tickets especially for spectators. You get to see the characters too!

Tip: Remember, the race day/weekend is your "Victory Lap!" You have trained for months and months and put in miles and miles with lots of blisters, sweat, and tears! This is your chance to enjoy everything. Don't rush; you probably aren't going to win. However, you will win memories of a lifetime. The races are experiences you will never forget! (Disney Podcaster & Marathoner Mike)

Tours

Disney offers a lot of different types of tours, but before you book, make sure to read this. Most tours at Disney are really geared towards adults or kids with excellent attention spans. The best part of the tours is hearing from the cast member experts and seeing behind the scenes. Some kids can appreciate this but it can also be kind of boring after riding Seven Dwarfs or walking through Toy Story Land. Keep that in mind if you are shelling out the extra bucks. Also, some tours don't allow photographs or phones so if your child can't part with their iPhone, Snapchat or other tech for more than 10 minutes, it may be best to forgo the tour.

PhotoPass Magic

In the world of Instagram and Snapchat, photos have become an even bigger part of a trip to WDW. PhotoPass photographers are everywhere. PhotoPass shots are increasing in popularity and there are sometimes lines for popular pics. Now, while you might think, "I'm not waiting in one more line, grandma can take the shot of us in front of the castle" just know that PhotoPass photographers have photo magic they add to your photos in post-production. These pictures are called Magic Shots.

Our family has had Magic Shots with Tinker Bell hanging out on our 18-year-old's hands, glowing creatures from Pandora overhead and even a video with Mickey. The kicker is that all of this magic is added after the photo is taken so you don't really know what you will get. And Disney likes to change this up, a lot. You can check the Disney PhotoPass Service Facebook page to find the Magic Shots that are happening around the parks. This is probably your best bet on what is going to be on offer while you are there as it does change. You may not get the exact photo or character listed, but you will get a great photo that doesn't have grandma's finger covering the lens.

> *Tip*: If you're looking for Magic Shots, find the pho-tographers that do not have their camera on a tripod. If they're holding the camera in their hand that's a good clue that they have Magic Shots available. You can also specifically ask the PhotoPass photographers if they have any Magic Shots and they are usually happy to give you one. (Disney blogger Serena)

If Magic Shots are your thing, definitely make sure to check out the info on PhotoPass Day in Appendix: Magical Tips

Mickey's Annual Parties

The mouse knows how to throw a party and your favorite char-acter(s) may be on the guest list. Mickey has two every year at Magic Kingdom: Mickey's Not-So-Scary Halloween Party and Mickey's Very Merry Christmas Party.

In this chapter I've included the overview of the events – the shows and parades, the cost, merchandise, all that good stuff. If a movie or character is on a treat, on merchandise, is dancing in a parade or show, or has a meet and greet at the party, I've gone through the painstaking process of adding it to that movie or character's own chapter.

Both parties are ticketed events at Magic Kingdom. Basically you buy a ticket in advance and then around 7 PM cast members have to be mean and start encouraging guests not going to the party to leave. As a partygoer you will typically have a bracelet that you pick up from a special stand in the park that identifies you as worthy and you get to stay.

Pricing in 2018 for the Halloween party ranged from $79 for an adult to $125 on Halloween night and for Christmas prices started at $95 and went up to $125 on the last night of the party, December 21st. The Christmas party is not held during the week of Christmas, as that is one of the busiest weeks of the year at Disney World. A child's ticket is only a few dollars cheaper and any child over 10 is considered an adult price ticket.

The parties only happen a few nights a week and they do sell out. The parties tend to be more crowded at the beginning and end of the season and on weekends. Weekdays are your best bet to experience the most during the party. If you only have a party ticket you can enter the park at 4 PM and the party goes from 7pm – midnight. If you have purchased a ticket to get into the parks you can enter the park before 4 PM.

The Halloween parties are on select nights starting mid-August until Halloween. Rumor is that the shows and Happy Hallowishes may be changing in 2019, but there will still be so much to do at this party that we need a list:

11 Reasons You Will Be Exhausted at the End of Mickey's Not-So Scary Halloween Party

1. Rides. With less folks in the park, lines are shorter. Oh and Haunted Mansion at the party is definitely a must. Not every attraction and restaurant is open during the party so make sure to check when booking if you have a "must" ride.

2. Attractions with a Halloween overlay. In 2018 Halloween effects were added to Mad Tea Party and Pirates of the Caribbean and Space Mountain had a spooky soundtrack. For 2019 the rumors are there will be overlays on Big Thunder Mountain, Tomorrowland Transit Authority PeopleMover and Monster Inc Laugh Floor.

3. Battle for the party exclusive Sorcerers of the Magic Kingdom card. The design changes every year to keep you coming back.

4. Dance Parties. At the Storybook Circus Disney Jr. Jam dance party Doc McStuffins and other Disney Jr. pals will be doing the Monster Mash. See actual monsters from Monsters Inc. showing off their dance moves at the Monstrous Scream-O-Ween Ball. George raises the roof, Sulley shakes it off and Mike leads a train (Disney version of a conga line).

5. A sing-along with all the other amuck maniacs at Hocus Pocus Villain Spelltacular Stage Show. This show has

dancing, spells, Halloween effects, the Sanderson sisters and they bring along some rarely seen in the parks Disney Villain friends. Previous shows had Oogie Boogie from *Nightmare Before Christmas*, Maleficent from *Sleeping Beauty* and Dr. Facilier from *Princess and the Frog*. The show happens multiple times in the evening during the party and is on the stage in front of Cinderella Castle. AP Jamie recommends seeing the first show "because you never know what will happen with Florida weather."

6. Happy Hallowishes. This 12-minute nighttime show is almost worth the cost of admission on its own and has moments that can actually be a bit scary. It's full of villains, villainous songs from the movies and Halloween specific fireworks. The fireworks are really the highlight of this show hosted by the Ghost Host from Haunted Mansion. Ursula, Jafar, Oogie Boogie and more help out with the soundtrack. In this show you will hear your favorite villains but not see them. There is a scream-along at the end and it can get loud, so consider yourself warned.

7. Mickey's Boo-To-You Halloween Parade. A very convincing Headless Horseman opens this celebration of all things spooky by riding down Main Street on an actual horse. Then Alice, princesses and a whole host of others dance down the street with whimsical masks on sticks. Pirates from the ride and movie, the evil stepsisters from *Cinderella*, and Oogie Boogie are just a few of the characters you will see. A whole lot of villains actually work together for an evil dance but the real highlight is seeing Haunted Mansion basically come to life with dancers from the ballroom scene and glowing floats.

8. Meeting characters. Villains and regular favorites in rare trick-or-treat ready characters are ready to meet and greet. Lines are long so most provide pre-printed autograph cards instead of signing your book. Meet Stitch as a superhero, hug Snow White and all seven Dwarfs, smell Lotso the Bear, or see the Fab Five in that year's costume. Just like you're picking your costume for that year's party, so are they and this is a unique opportunity

to get your favorite mouse or duck dressed as a pumpkin, knight or witch. Winnie the Pooh and friends have also been known to pull on their costumes for the party. The characters, especially the villains and rare characters at the party can change so definitely check the My Disney experience app. *Tip*: Don't forget your costume! This party is also one of the few times of year adults can wear costumes in the park. But Disney is Disney and there are rules. The guidelines are strict and it's important to follow them because it may impact getting in the park. You can't have anything covering your entire body. Be careful of having stuff that dangles off you if you plan to go on rides. But most of all don't forget its Florida. It's hot. Don't layer too much. (AP Jamie)

9. PhotoPass Magic Shots. There are a few party exclusives including the Headless Horseman, the hitchhiking ghosts from Haunted Mansion and some gravediggers. The Magic Shot locations are noted on the party map.

10. Seasonal treats. The treats change each year but a 2018 highlight was the Hitchhiking ghosts dessert that had a chocolate with the ghosts on it and the entire dessert looked like they were in a doom buggy. See the party map for the specific locations, as every treat is not available at every location. The other way to get a sugar rush at the party is to trick or treat.

11. Shopping. This party is so full of merchandise you can only get during the party there is too much to list. Here are a few highlights. There is always a shirt usually an ornament with Mickey and Minnie, pins with villains and a line of *Hocus Pocus* items. In 2018 there was a super wicked cauldron mug and other Sanderson sisters goodies to celebrate the 25th anniversary of the film.

This will be a jam-packed 5 hours and you're not likely to be able to see every show, visit every character, eat every treat and buy every piece of merchandise. There are some great blogs about a plan of attack for this party to try and see as much as possible. Most experts say to not waste time going on rides if you want to see all the shows and visit a lot of characters. The character lines do get long so be ready to prioritize. Others love the fact that the ride lines are so short and try to cram in as many as possible.

Figure out what, and who is most important to you. And then be okay if your entire plan is blown to smithereens because you see Snow White and all seven Dwarfs and who can pass that up! One thing I definitely recommend is to just take a few moments to wander around, take in all the decorations, the spooky vibe, check out all the creative costumes of your fellow party-goers, and hug your favorite ghost or goblin.

Now, to Christmas. Mickey's Very Merry Christmas parties (let's called it Mickey's Christmas Party for short) start in early November and go until a few days before Christmas. Magic Kingdom is also the park to visit for Christmas cheer even if you are not there during the party.

Warning, the week of Christmas-New Years is the busiest time of year at Disney World. Parks can even hit capacity and have to turn guests away. Disney chooses to reward those that brave the parks during this week with some of the party exclusive entertainment. If the Must See is exclusive to the party or Christmas week, I've noted it in the list.

15 Must Sees During the Holiday Season at Magic Kingdom.

1. Jingle Cruise. This is the Jungle Cruise with a very festive overlay. Even the queue is full of holiday cheer.

2. Holiday merchandise. Every year there is a new design for shirts, ornaments and of course, that years exclusive Ugly Christmas Sweater. There is also party exclusive merchandise typically including ears, shirts, ornaments and pins. A great free party souvenir is the party map. The design changes every year and is a festive keepsake. *Tip*: During the week of Christmas-New Year's stores will have any remaining party merchandise on clearance

3. Hear the holiday cheer. From the festive tunes playing down Main Street to the Dapper Dans singing holiday favorites.

4. Sorcerers of the Magic Kingdom Mickey's Christmas Party exclusive card. The design changes every year to

keep you coming back. Past years have seen Rover from the Carousel of Progress attraction, Olaf's Snowgies and festive Goofy.

5. Free cookies and festive drinks including a Sno-cone, Santa cookie and a Santa pretzel during Mickey's Christmas Party

6. Club Tinsel dance party. Ever wondered what reindeer do in the off-season? Dancing may be on the list. Reindeer and Pluto has been known to come by and cut a rug for a few at this party. During Mickey's Christmas Party and week of Christmas.

7. Elsa freezing the castle during the Frozen Holiday Wish show at Cinderella Castle.

8. Totally Tomorrowland Christmas Show. Hang out for the whole show to see festive Mike Wazowski and Sulley from *Monsters Inc.* and Santa Stitch. During Mickey's Christmas Party and week of Christmas.

9. Mickeys Most Merriest Celebration at Cinderella Castle. I'll be honest; the content of this show is random. There is a song about texting and then a bit later the Caballeros show up and do a little Tis the Season en Español. There are a ton of characters mashed into it from Alice to Woody playing guitar and Clarabelle even channels her inner Mariah with "All I Want For Christmas is You." The best moment though is when Clarabelle declares "more cowbell!" During Mickey's Christmas Party and week of Christmas.

10. *Mickey's Christmas Carol* windows at the Emporium shop. These are a real treat to see. *Tip*: hang out until after the last nighttime show and Main Street has cleared out to really take your time to check out the amazing details in these window displays.

11. Once Upon a Christmastime Parade. All of the characters are in their scarves and holiday finest. Anna and Elsa are in an actual sleigh pulled by real horses while Ralph and Vanellope are on Christmas candy floats and Mary Poppins and Bert even do a little dance down Main Street. During Mickey's Christmas Party. The week of Christmas

you can actually see the parade during the day. It's a very different experience and you can pick up a lot of details not easy to see at night, like Olaf, who is so nicely dressed.

12. Special character meet and greets. Traditional favorites in holiday fashions or rare characters including Jack Skellington as Sandy Claws, Scrooge McDuck and lumberjack Donald and Mary Poppins with Bert. Sometimes even a few penguins pop by. During Mickey's Christmas Party. Tip: the lines for many rare characters can be very long. I tried to visit Sandy Claws at 1045 PM only to be told the line was still 45 minutes long. Also, most characters do not do autographs during the party. Cast members hand out pre-printed cards with autographs instead.

13. PhotoPass magic shots. Zero by Haunted Mansion (Mickey's party exclusive) to holiday Tinker Bell in front of the castle. Speaking of the castle...

14. Holiday Wishes the nighttime fireworks show. Watch the castle transform to Christmas candy, a Christmas tree and an explosion of color. This show features a ton of fireworks. 12 straight minutes of fireworks hosted by Jiminy Cricket with a special surprise from Tinker Bell. The ending is spectacular with fireworks surrounding you on almost all sides. During Mickey's Christmas Party and week of Christmas.

15. The decorations. Stand on Main Street with the snow falling, the castle dripping in icicles in front of you with a giant tree behind you and just take in all the sights and sounds of Christmas. Hopefully you are with some of the ones you love most and can give them a tired smile and a hug and as Elsa says, "feel the Christmas spirit in the air."

You will need some Santa magic and probably multiple trips to the park and Mickey's Christmas parties trips to see every show, visit every character, eat every treat and buy every piece of merchandise. There are some great blogs about a plan of attack for this party to try and see as much as possible.

You have to really figure out what and who is most important to you. And then be okay if your entire plan is blown to smithereens because you see Judy Hopps and who can pass that up! One thing I definitely recommend is to just take a few moments to wander around, see decorations and just try to take it all in. Except the snow on Main Street. Just admire it. Don't take that in. It's soap and doesn't taste so good.

Epcot Festivals

There are four festivals now that feature artsy, Christmassy, flowery and even foodie ways to play with your favorite movies and characters at Epcot. They are more than just food -- though the food is the best part! You can get all the delicious details on the festivals in my book Tasting the Magic from A-Z. In that book you will get detailed information on each festival, tips on maximizing your time, what you can see, hear and eat and recommended dishes and cocktails from the food kiosks.

To avoid going into the details of every festival in every entry in this book, I'm including the general details here. Oh, and you know that Disney loves change disclaimer I've mentioned previously? Yep, that applies here too. Entertainment, food, gardens, character art, etc. do change up a little every year so make sure to check your Epcot Festival passport or ask a cast member when you arrive. It may just be that the shrimp and grits are at a different food kiosk or the Mickey topiary has moved!

Most Epcot festivals have some sort of scavenger hunt featuring a character. To play you pay about $10 to purchase a map and set of stickers. Then hunt around the festival for the character hidden around World Showcase. Use your map and stickers to keep track and then take your map to a redemption station to get a prize. The prizes tend to change each year. Past hunters have gone home with Figment pins, gardener Minnie patches, Remy & Chef Mickey cups and Chip & Dale pins

For Festival of the Arts it's typically Figment's Brush with the Masters. Flower and Garden had a new hunt in 2018 with Spike's Pollen Nation Exploration, featuring the adorable little bee that annoyed Donald and Pluto in cartoons from the 40's and 50's. Food and Wine is Remy with Remy's Ratatouille Hide & Squeak. Festival of the Holidays has been Chip & Dales Christmas Tree spree.

Epcot International Festival of the Arts

Festival of the Arts runs from January until February. This is the newest of the four festivals and is steadily growing in popularity. If you don't like the Orlando heat, this is a good time to visit Disney World. Festival of the Arts brings the magic to visual, culinary and performing arts.

The highlights are crafters and artists dotted around the park with unique merchandise for purchase. My favorite is the Disney custom-painted Toms shoes. For entertainment there's the Disney on Broadway concert series where you can hear famous Broadway stars perform Disney classics. Dotted everywhere are living portraits, a giant paint-by numbers community art piece, chalk art and custom portraits of characters. But my favorite part of any Epcot festival is the food and this fest does not disappoint. Festival of the Arts has food kiosks called Food Studios that offer over 30 culinary masterpieces and grown-up beverages. I definitely recommend the Deconstructed BLT, the Pop-Artsicle, Pop't Art and Popping Bubbles Cocktail.

Epcot International Flower & Garden Festival

Flower & Garden is the springtime festival running from March-May. Flower & Garden plays on all of your senses with larger than life topiaries, fragrant blooms, the Garden Rocks concert series and edible flowers. I've included information on the movie-and-character-specific topiaries that are growing around the park in the relevant chapters.

The food at Flower & Garden is at food kiosks called Outdoor Kitchens and they are home to some of my favorite festival dishes; the Instagram-famous Violet Lemonade, walking-friendly sugar cane shrimp skewers and the maple popcorn shake.

Every year about 10-20 topiaries from Flower & Garden stay up and are decorated for the other festivals. Stitch, Mickey and Minnie are just a few getting festive with Santa hats for Festival of the Holidays and Mickey grilling out at Food and Wine. Just one more thing to check on the festival map.

Epcot International Food & Wine Festival

Food & Wine is the most popular of the four festivals. Thousands of Disney fans flock to Epcot to taste and drink their way around the world. In addition to more than 200 different food and drinks to try you can enjoy the Eat to the Beat concert series. There are some big names in these shows. Past shows have included some favorites for this child of the 90's -- Boyz II Men, Hanson and 98 Degrees. But the reason to come to Food & Wine is the food kiosks, called Marketplaces. There are too many delicious dishes to list here but a few of the highlights include: avocado crema, spicy hummus fries and the famous Ice Pop in France.

A place to make sure you stop for more than just the delicious smells is the Chocolate Experience in the festival center. Each year there are outstanding chocolate sculptures featuring things Disney is excited about for that year. The details these chocolatiers can put into chocolate is amazing and worth a visit. Past years have included the house from UP, Toy Story Land, and Nightmare Before Christmas. You should definitely go and take peek because you never know when you can see your favorite movie in a whole new way.

Every year there are festival exclusive pins. Because I am a total foodie and Epcot World Showcase is my favorite part of Disney World, I think the 2018 Mystery Pins are definitely worth a mention. There were 11 pins in total one for each of the World Showcase pavilions. Each pin featured a character enjoying a food related to that land. Remy is enjoying ratatouille in France, Mushu is slurping noodles in China and Abu is munching on bread in Morocco. The merchandising minds at Disney are just so clever -- and that is why they get all my money.

Epcot International Festival of the Holidays

Festival of the Holidays is just one more reason to visit Disney World when it's most magical. This festival starts at the tail end of Food & Wine in late November and runs until late December. Festival of the Holidays will take you into the holidays in many different countries: from the decorations, to storytellers, to music and of course food.

The food kiosks are aptly named Holiday Kitchens and visiting them is like having friends in each country that invite you over to a traditional holiday meal. France has the traditional Buche Noel while the American pavilion features a turkey dinner with all the trimmings. There are entire Holiday Kitchens devoted to sweet treats and in 2018 there was even a cookie walk.

Resorts

Stay in *Little Mermaid* themed-rooms, see a gigantor Woody statue, and swim in a Three Caballeros pool. Venture beyond the parks and see what magic is hiding at the many Disney resort hotels.

A number of resorts are undergoing major refurbishment at the time of publication and new resorts are being built. The information included on the following resorts may change once the construction is complete: All-Star Movies, Music and Sports, Animal Kingdom Lodge, Caribbean Beach, Coronado Springs, Old Key West Resort and Saratoga Springs.

There are magical displays worth a special trip at some resorts during the holidays and many are mentioned in the Seasonal section of applicable chapters. Each resort will have a Christmas tree and decorations themed to the resort. There are also displays that tend to change but are worth doing a little research.

Some of my favorite holiday decorations seen on previous trips include: Elsa's castle in gingerbread at the Contemporary, Tink on snowflake shaped sign at Port Orleans French Quarter, wreaths decorated by Cast Members based on their favorite movies at the All Star Resorts, Chef Mickey in a detailed holiday kitchen all in miniature and chocolate at Boardwalk, and my favorite, the gingerbread carousel at Beach Club. Previous carousel themes have included Lilo & Stitch and Donald and Daisy Duck. You could lose an hour taking in all the details and delicious smells.

Seasonal

Some characters, especially the villains, have certain times of year they tend to come and hang at Walt Disney World. This section will include seasonal shows and special seasonal treats not included in the other lists or the Mickey's Parties section. If you are like me and think that Christmas at Disney is the most magical time of year, make sure to check Seasonal,

Mickey's Parties and the Epcot International Festival of the Holidays in Epcot Festivals when in the chapter for your favorite movie or character.

Spring

In spring Epcot is the place to be with the Egg-stravaganza Easter egg hunt. Similar to the Epcot festival scavenger hunts you buy your map and stickers for around $10. You search for all the eggs and then take your completed map to get what I think is one of the best hunt prizes, a character Easter egg. This hunt typically runs from mid-March to around Easter. The hunt and prize eggs have had classic characters Minnie, Mickey, Goofy and also rare characters like Perry the Platypus, Mike and Sulley from *Monsters, Inc.* and Thumper from *Bambi*. The characters on the prize eggs—and on the eggs you're searching for -- may change but this is really fun activity to do with kids of all ages.

Summer

If you're at Disney World in summer, one fun activity that might help you cool off a bit is Christmas in July. Disney releases a line of Christmas merchandise and starts sharing details about the upcoming Holiday season. What is truly neat about this event is the characters that can be found at different resorts.

In 2018 Santa Mickey and Mrs. Claus Minnie made a visit to All-Star Sports while holiday Donald and Daisy visited Old Key West Resort. Donald and Daisy's costumes were excellent. Donald had a green tunic with striped edging that looked like a candy cane. He also had a fuzzy red hat with a pom-pom. Daisy had a red tunic with the same striped edging. They looked like they owned a holiday candy store and took a break to hug customers in front a Christmas tree.

Winter

Probably before you've managed to put your Halloween costume away, Disney World is getting ready for the holidays. Christmas-time at Disney World is incredibly magical and every year they add more reasons to visit. There are almost two Holiday seasons at Disney; Nov 1 until the week of the Christmas holiday and then Christmas Eve through New Year's Day.

The reason I say this, is the week of Christmas through New Year's is one of the single busiest weeks of the year. On New Year's Eve day the Magic Kingdom has hit capacity. Capacity is a lot of people. I would not recommend being at Disney World unless you love being around thousands and thousands of people, waiting in really long lines, or this is the only week you can possibly visit Disney World.

Magic Kingdom

The resort and park decorations are all typically up in November. You don't have to attend Mickey's Very Merry Christmas Party to experience the beauty of Cinderella Castle drenched in icicles. Check out the list: "15 Reasons to Visit Magic Kingdom During the Holidays."

One of my favorite wintertime activities is looking at all the detail in the Christmas trees at each park and resort. "Cast members decorate more than 1,500 trees during the holidays," shares Theme park author Alexa. These trees vary from a holiday tree at Be Our Guest, which is right in front of the windows so it appears to be snowing right behind the tree to over 20 movie and character-inspired tree at Disney Springs Tree Trail.

Epcot

This park has an entire International Festival of the Holidays this time of year. Read more about in the Epcot Festivals.

Hollywood Studios

Every park has their own way of celebrating the holidays and at Hollywood Studios it's called Flurry of Fun. The festivities include a special nighttime show Jingle Bell Jingle Jam, holiday decorations around the park, a visit with Santa and the best part, Sunset Seasons Greetings.

Jingle Bell Jingle Jam is a nighttime show with projections onto Grauman's Chinese Theatre. The show is about 15 minutes long and has fireworks, lasers, trees that look as if they are sparkling and a festive storyline to find Santa featuring characters from *Prep and Landing*. This show has a lot going on and features a clip from almost every Disney movie with a winter or Christmas scene.

Trying to catch everything or the brief moment your favorite movie or character is in the show can be exhausting. It's almost like watching a tennis match! Try to stand a bit further back for this show as there are screens next to the theatre. I'll be honest. I'm not a huge fan. Trying to take everything in after a long day in the parks is a lot for your brain. I'd prefer if the clips were a little bit longer and switched more slowly. But if you love Disney holiday films, this is a must-see show.

There is a Dessert Party for this show, which can go a long way in getting a good viewing spot. There are festive holiday treats, fun cocktails and a special holiday character that visits the party. There is no guarantee who it will be, but Santa Goofy has been on the guest list. The cost has historically been about $80 for an adult. If you're a huge Prep and Landing fan it may be worth the money for you but I think Minnie's Holiday Dine is a probably a better use of your food budget.

Another nighttime show at Hollywood Studios is Sunset Seasons Greetings. On Sunset Boulevard billboards come alive with holiday scenes. But what is truly mind-blowing is the use of projections to transform the Tower of Terror into a festival, playful show with Disney and Pixar favorites. There are four different portions of the show that start with an opening scene on the billboards and then the projections on the Tower of Terror. There are scenes for *Toy Story*, *Olaf's Frozen Adventure*, the Muppets, and *Mickey's Christmas Carol*. To see them all, plan to hang out for about 15 minutes.

> *Tip*: If you want to see the amazing detail of the projections try and stand close to the Tower of Terror. Just make sure you have a view of the billboards.

Hollywood Studios was once home to one of the most epic holiday displays at Disney with the Osborne lights display. With the new lands for Toy Story and Star Wars this display went away. Fans were not thrilled and missed having something festive in this park.

Star Wars Galaxy's Edge may not be getting a Christmas Tree but Toy Story Land had a lot of holiday cheer. The giant character statues are dressed up for the season with Woody in a scarf and Rex with reindeer antlers. The Rex, Jessie and Woody soundtrack near the land entrance has a few holiday lines sprinkled in. There are giant green alien ornament decorations and the Alien Swirling Saucers ride had a few holiday songs mixed into the standard soundtrack. There are also subtle easy to miss decorations around the land. Can you find the Angel Kitty ornament? Angel Kitty was in *Toy Story That Time Forgot* and her ornament looks like Andy made it with macaroni noodles and gold spray paint.

Animal Kingdom

Animal Kingdom is decorated for the holidays and has multiple trees featuring handmade ornaments. There is a Diwali version of the UP! Great Bird Adventure show. The holidays overall are a bit more subdued at Animal Kingdom. It's nice to have somewhere to go to have a break from the festiveness, if needed.

Resorts

A free activity during this time of year is wandering the resorts to take in all the decorations and gingerbread displays. Every resort will have decorations and a Christmas tree themed to the resort.

In the past the All-Star resorts have even hosted a cast member wreath-decorating contest. You can find some rare movies in the wreaths, as there is usually a Nightmare Before Christmas, Marvel or Star Wars fan in the group. Some resorts go even further with model trains, giant gingerbread houses and carousels made of sugar.

Disney Springs

Another fun free holiday activity is to visit The Tree Trail at Disney Springs. Here you can see Christmas trees inspired by movies and characters that are perfectly decorated. This event is becoming really popular and Disney is responding by decorating 25 trees for the 2018 trail.

There are trees for Mickey & Minnie and Beauty and the Beast but you may also find Pluto, Mulan and even Robin Hood. Each tree is uniquely decorated with clever references to the films and characters.

It's fun to simply examine the trees and find all the subtle references like a dinglehopper on the Little Mermaid tree or a magic mirror on the Villains tree. This tree was the location of DVC Sarah's favorite PhotoPass photo at Disney World. Like

Sarah, I'm a big fan of the Disney Villains tree with its' festive references to Ursula, the Evil Queen and even Gaston.

The coolest part of the tree trail is you can actually get up close to the trees and see all the details. The decorations tend to stay the same year to year. The details I include in the book are from the trees in 2018 and 2017 so see what new surprises you can find when you visit. There are so many details and clever references it's hard to see them all. I keep waiting for a Scavenger Hunt like Remy's Hide and Squeak just for the tree trail. You can visit from early November through early January.

Sprinkling of Pixie Dust

The Sprinkling of Pixie Dust section has those little extras that didn't fit in one of the other categories. Facts, rumors and magical memories are just a few of the types of things you may find in this section. Some movies and characters have so much pixie dust around Walt Disney World that I didn't even need to include this section for them!

9 of the Most Photo-Worthy Fab Five Costumes

1. Pluto's Halloween costume. He dresses up as a vampire and I think it is just adorable. – Theme Park Author Alexa

2. I love meeting Madam Daisy Fortuna and the Great Goofini at Pete's Silly Side Show in Storybook Circus. A fortuneteller is such a fitting act for Daisy. Her costume is rich and ornate as well as simply fabulous. – DCP Anna

3. I am a sucker for Mickey and his classic tux with the yellow bowtie. You can find him at Epcot Character Spot wearing that outfit. – Disney Blogger Serena

4. Mickey in his Hawaii garb over at the Lilo & Stitch Ohana breakfast at the Polynesian Resort – Disney Podcaster Mike

5. Mickey as a preppy vampire at Minnie's Halloween Dine. I love Halloween. – CM Nick. Find this Mickey at Minnie's Halloween Dine at Hollywood Studios.

6. Goofy in a Santa Suit at Minnie's Holiday Dine at Hollywood Studios – DVC Dawn. You can also find Santa

Goofy at a meet and greet at Hollywood Studios, Animal Kingdom and during Mickey's Very Merry Christmas Party at Magic Kingdom.

7. My favorite meet and greet is at Red Carpet Dreams in Hollywood Studios. In just one spot, you can meet Minnie and Mickey in the most adorable outfits. Minnie is dolled up in the cutest 1920s inspired dress and Mickey looks the part of the Sorcerer's Apprentice. – DCP Anna

8. The Christmas and Halloween Minnie's Seasonal Dines are both awesome. - DVC Sarah. The characters all have special outfits at this event! You can see Witch Minnie and Mickey in a festive red jacket with peppermint swirl candy buttons.

9. I love the space and outfit for Daisy as part of the Donald's Dino Bash at Animal Kingdom. This is Disney storytelling at its best with Daisy playing fashion designer and then having a space and a costume that reflects her new profession.

APPENDIX B

Magical Tips

I had the opportunity to interview so many excellent people for this book who are serious Disney fans. Some of them have worked or currently work at Disney. Others run at Disney a lot, and one has even visited Disney more times than the number of years she has been alive. As you can imagine, they have so much good information and useful tips for you. This is a list of magical and useful info that will help you in your search for your favorite movie or character that just didn't fit somewhere else.

- "If you can't find a character you're looking for, stop by guest services. They have a master list that they can look up and find out what characters are appearing in any of the parks that week," says Disney Blogger Serena.

- "If there is a character that is part of a show but doesn't have a meet and greet, it's always possible to make that opportunity happen for yourself. Asking cast members in a friendly manner never hurts!" advises DCP Anna.

- Cast members are some of the biggest Disney fans out there. Talking to a cast member is always a good idea. "Ask cast members any questions you want. You get a lot of information from them," suggests DVC Sarah. Even if they can't hook you up with a character, they may know a fun fact, give you the inside scoop on special merchandise or a show, or they may have a magical story. Many of my most unexpected magical Disney moments happened because I talked to a cast member.

"When you're meeting a character, think about the character's movie/show and talk to them about what happened in the films. It will add to the experience and make it more fun for everybody," says theme park author Alexa. Disney Blogger Serena also suggests that you wear things that represent your favorite characters. Maybe it's a pair of themed mouse ears or T-shirt, or accessories like a cute bag, or maybe you can go all the way and actually DisneyBound as a specific character. Not only is it fun, but if you do happen to run across that character, they know immediately that you're a big fan and will focus their attention on you. This makes for some fun engagement.

 Is finding characters at the top of your Disney to do list? Then there are a few events that you might want to attend. These are considered the ultimate experiences for seeing rare characters, seeing characters in different costumes or seeing them in a whole new way. DVC Dawn recommends the DVC Membership Magic event, "We were able to see Jesse, Woody and Bullseye together." AP Jamie recommends the many Annual Passholder events that happen each year, "Ask everywhere for discounts and for many events, there are special AP gifts." In the past these have included an AP Food and Wine button with Remy and a Festival of the Arts print with Belle. Do you have a Chase Disney Visa? There's also a special Character Spot at Epcot and Hollywood Studios at Star Wars Launch Bay. The spot at Epcot has a rotation of characters between Mickey, Minnie, Goofy or Pluto.

 "If you're looking for magic shots, notice the photographers that don't have their camera on a tripod. If they're holding the camera in their hand, that's a good clue that they have Magic Shots available. You can also specifically ask the PhotoPass photographers if they have any magic shots and are usually happy to give you one," recommends Disney Blogger Serena. You can also check the Disney PhotoPass Service Facebook page to find the magic shots currently on offer.

🐭 For the ultimate PhotoPass day, visit Disney on August 19. This is World Photo Day and is also PhotoPass Day at Disney World. It started in 2016 and each year the offerings keep getting better. This day has props from movies, extremely rare magic shots and even rarer character meet and greets. The event takes place at all four parks and Disney Springs. In 2018 a few of the standouts were: character meet and greets with Bolt, Cruella de Vil, Jafar, Pinocchio and Geppetto; Props including Russell's Grape Soda bottle cap pin prop, *Beauty and the Beast* light painting and Mickey Pretzel prop; the Magic Shots Kevin from *UP*, Rizzo from the *Muppets* and my favorite the Baby Groot Magic Shot. Only time will tell what future years will bring but clear out your photos and plan for a four-park day. There are even special Magic Shots at Disney Springs so add one more stop on your photo filled day.

🐭 "Always be on the look out for interesting characters at the World Gateway locations at EPCOT. Smaller, more intimate meet and greets often occur around World Showcase with seemingly random characters. It's a good place to warm up familiar faces. This is why you'll often see some of your favorite characters that typically come out only during Halloween start to pop up during the summer," advised DCP Anna. On a trip in 2013 our family experienced this magic and my son Oliver was able to meet Mickey, Donald, Goofy's son Max, Pinocchio, and even Gideon, one of the bad guys from *Pinocchio*. All in about 15 minutes.

🐭 AP Jamie suggests: "Character-Palooza! Is a top-secret meet and greet that helps characters- in-training practice with meeting guests." This is a fairly well kept secret and Disney likes to keep the element of surprise so the location tends to change but is usually at Hollywood Studios. Sometimes you'll be wandering around Tower of Terror or Streets of America and suddenly, bam! There are characters! The guest list is never a guarantee but here are a few characters that have been spotted in the past: Mary Poppins and Bert, Mushu from *Mulan*, Pinocchio and even Robin Hood (the Disney version, not Kevin Costner.)

Mary Poppins Returns, the opening of *Star Wars:* Galaxy's Edge, *Frozen 2,* Mickey Mouse turns 90, the 50ᵗʰ anniversary of the opening of Walt Disney World are just a few of the many major milestones coming up. Disney Parks love to have something to celebrate. This includes character birthdays, park opening anniversaries, movie releases and milestones, you name it, Disney World will likely have some sort of celebration for it. These celebrations can be huge with parties that take over whole lands in the parks or small with cupcakes or PhotoPass Magic Shots. Here are just a few ways the Disney experts and I have seen Disney World celebrate in the past:

Release of *Incredibles 2*: 2018 was an Incredibles Summer at Disney World. Party goers got super at Glow Dance Parties, munched on "Edna Mode No Capes Just Crepes" sundaes, had a dance party with characters from the films, got a PhotoPass Magic Shot with Jack Jack shooting lasers from his eyes and so much more super stuff.

Frozen Summer Fun had special parades, Olaf cupcakes and even the Frozen Summer Games with Olaf and Sven at Blizzard Beach. The most epic was Wandering Oaken's Trading Post & Frozen Funland where you could ice skate at Disney World. In the summer. In central Florida. If any of you readers have been to Florida you know the magic involved in making ice skating in the middle of a steaming hot, humid swamp possible.

The *Peter Pan* vault release in 2018 was celebrated with the return of the Peter's shadow Magic Shot, a small *Peter Pan* Disneybounding parade and the release of the *Peter Pan* ice cream float.

"Whenever a new Disney movie comes out, Disney Springs will often have large cutouts, backdrops, or other photo spots near the AMC Theater," recommends DCP Anna.

My favorite has to be the Donald Duck 50ᵗʰ Anniversary parade in 1984. "They had lives ducks in party hats on the float with Donald!" recalls AP Jamie.

One of the most memorable celebrations for me was the 25ᵗʰ anniversary of Walt Disney World with the theme "Remember the Magic". The celebration actually ran for over a year and included an all-new parade, the return of Spectromagic and a lot more. But the thing most Disney fans will never forget was the transformation of Cinderella Castle to a giant pink birthday cake. Seriously. I saw it with my own two eyes. This was in 1996, before Facebook and Instagram and most people didn't even have a computer at home, let alone in their pocket. So that means guests traveling from all over the world to see the icon of Walt Disney World were pretty surprised to find a gigantic balloon covered pink birthday cake instead of an elegant princess castle.

Disney celebrates with sugar and merchandise. Seriously. For every anniversary, party, movie release, whatever the occasion, there will be some sort of special treat. For Epcot's 35th anniversary there was the Spaceship Earth Cupcake topped with about 3 inches of silver frosting that really looked like Spaceship Earth. Animal Kingdom's 20th anniversary? A Tree of Life inspired cupcake. Hollywood Studios 25th? A chocolate cupcake topped with a pile of frosting, Mickey sprinkles and a memorable chocolate decoration of Mickey.

Every park at Disney World has a Starbucks and these tend to be the home to a lot of the special event cupcakes. Each Starbucks location has a park-friendly name so they can be tricky to find on the map. The Olaf cupcake in summer has been spotted at Main Street Bakery in Magic Kingdom, while Spaceship Earth is at the Fountain View in Epcot. Trolley Car Café in Hollywood Studios had the super chocolate *Solo: A Star Wars Story* cupcake while Creature Comforts at Animal Kingdom has had the Cotton Top Tamarin cupcake. While celebrating at Disney adds on the pounds, it also lightens your wallet with the other magical celebration must have...

Disney celebrates with sugar and merchandise. T-shirts, key chains, magnets, ears, stickers and never forget...the pins. There must always be pins. A great way to find merchandise in the parks for your favorite movie or character is to go into the Shop Disney Parks app (the app not shopdisney.com). Search the movie or character you are looking for and then you can see merchandise on maps of the park, letting you know which stores have your items in stock. This is also an excellent way to find stores that may have special items or merchandise with rarely seen characters. The DisneyStyle store at Disney Springs opened in 2018 and had an attraction line of merchandise with the Country Bears and even Mr. Toad.

Disney loves merchandise so much they have Merchandise Events. Yep. This is a thing. Go over to Disneyworld.com and search on merchandise events. There is a complete list of the active and future events listed. These can include exclusive launches of toys like Funko Pops; Pin releases; artist showcases with Disney animators, artists and authors and even jewelry and fashion trunk shows. This is a unique way to celebrate spending money with fellow fans and possibly to meet some of the people behind the souvenirs we love. The events take place all over the parks and quite a few happen at Disney Springs. I definitely recommend taking a peek at this page when planning your trip to see if there is anything special planned.

Do some window-shopping on Main Street in Magic Kingdom, on Hollywood and Sunset Boulevards in Hollywood Studios and in Disney Springs. There are different displays throughout the year at many locations that are fun to see. Walt always advocated for the parks to be kid-friendly and had the shop windows in all the parks put lower to the ground so kids can easily see inside. Daisy was baking up sweet treats in the window of Main Street Confectionery in Magic Kingdom. I have seen a Christmas-themed Minnie kick line at Hollywood Studios. Also at Hollywood Studios is AP Jamie's favorite window. It's at the hat shop and is a poster for *Johnny Fedora* and *Alice Blue Bonnet*, which are her all-time favorite shorts. If you are looking for homage to a Disney classic, check out the hat shop window.

Here is a way to get all exclusive drawings of your favorite Fab Five characters (and Chip & Dale)! In 2018 the Epcot Kidcot Fun Stops got a makeover courtesy of Ziploc. Yep. That Ziploc. You know the bags you would love to have to put your phone in during the middle of a random Florida monsoon. As of the launch in 2018 there were 11 of these stops, one in each of the main pavilions.

At your first stop you will be given a handy dandy Ziploc bag made to look like an old fashioned suitcase. Don't let the kid in the name of this fool you. These are cool. You get stickers, booklets, fun drawings with your favorite characters to color and you can chat with cast members from the countries. This is honestly the best part.

You can be chatting with the cast members about London, Paris or Shanghai while decorating the cards that go with each country. One side of the card has a little information about the country and a space with the prompt *Make a new friend*. It's in this area you and your new cast member friend can have a little artsy fun.

The other side of the card is a drawing that you can color and decorate. The drawing is of some of the most beloved Disney characters in different country relevant activities. Daisy is getting royal in the UK with Goofy and Donald as her knights. Minnie and Daisy are drumming in China. Mickey and Minnie are atop the Statue of Liberty on the card in the American Pavilion Kidcot Stop. My favorite is Chip n Dale making off with a pretzel in Germany.

I will miss the cool Day of the Dead sugar masks that were the most recent Mexico Kidcot stop but it was time for a change and a drawing of Donald whacking a piñata is a fairly decent substitute.

Now this new Kidcot experience just started. Over time I fully expect Disney to add new cards. Maybe Mulan and Mushu in China, Pinocchio in Italy or *Coco* in Mexico.

Acknowledgments

Did you know if you look in the My Disney Experience app late at night it says: "Shh...Characters are Sleeping." That app was one of many sources of information on where to find the characters and movies in all their different forms in and around the Walt Disney World Resort.

Magic and pixie dust to all the Disney fans out there behind the blogs, books, and podcasts and who are a constant source of information and inspiration—especially to my friends over at the Mouse Knows Best Podcast (TMKB). It was the TMKB team who helped trigger the idea for this book by mentioning the princess-inspired royal guest rooms at Port Orleans Riverside in one of their episodes.

Giant Oliver & Company thanks to Julie and being the Disney phone-a-friend. Boxes of sake level gratitude to my Disney Bestie and fellow author Jamie Nelson (@lilo_thelostprincess) for being kind, supportive and all-knowing about most things Disney. And always willing to share that genius, even at 1 in the morning!

Multiple magical people allowed me to interview them and share the unique ways they love to immerse themselves in their favorite Disney stories. They shared so many helpful tips, history and magic. Find them sprinkled throughout the book.

- Alexa, author of the series *Disney Till You're Dizzy*. These books are bursting with fun facts, rumors and myths about Walt Disney World and Disneyland. She has been to Disney Parks more times than she can count. She knows over 2,002 facts about Disney World and is sharing a few of those in this book but make sure to check out her books to get your Disney trivia fix. Just look for Theme Park Author Alexa to find all her tips and magic.

- Anna, the resident Disney College Program (DCP) expert. She is a lifelong Disney fan has been in the DCP and was asked back to be in the DCP Alumni program and spent an incredible summer working at Disney World during 2018. Anna was honored to work in Hollywood Studios during the opening of Toy Story Land and to herd Padawans during the Jedi Training. Ever wonder where all those magical stories behind the attractions, shows, and even the signage at Disney World are from? It's created by a Walt Disney Imagineering Show Writers and Anna's goal is to one day be one of those Imagineering brains behind the magical stories you experience at Disney Parks. Find all her great tips and stories with DCP Anna

- Jamie, the Annual Passholder (AP) expert. Look for AP Jamie tips & magic. See her magical Disney photos of Disney World and Disneyland on Instagram @lilo_the-lostprincess. Also keep your eye out for a book on dining on Disneyland from this talented, food-loving Disney fan.

- Mike is the host of the popular Disney podcast Be Our Guest and is also a certified Disney planner with Magic for Less Travel. Mike is an avid runner and the source of all the marathon expertise. Look for Disney Podcaster Mike Tips to find all the great info from Mike.

- Nick is the true expert as a full-time Disney cast member. He grew up in the Orlando area and both he and his wife work for Disney, Nick in a corporate role and his wife in the parks. You definitely want to look for all the magic he brings with Cast Member Nick tips and info.

- Sarah and Dawn are mother daughter Disney superfans and Disney Vacation Club (DVC) members. As of 2018 Dawn has visited Disney World 40+ times and Sarah 12 times and her first trip was when she was just 4. Sarah has been to Disney more times than the years she's been alive! Look for DVC Sarah and Dawn for their family travel tips and info.

- Serena is the luckiest person on the list because she lives only 10 minutes from the magic of Walt Disney World. As you can imagine she is a wealth of knowledge and shares that knowledge on her blog livingbyDisney.com on Instagram @livingbydisney and as a contributor to WDW Magazine. Look for Disney Blogger Serena to see all the goodies from a true local.

Thanks to my own Fab Five my kids Oliver, Austin, Annie, Maggie and Nate. Also, to our extended Fab Five: Nick and Sam. Fans of my books will know Sam as the illustrator in my first two books. She is super talented so make sure to check those out.

Shout out to my Dad who surprised me with the first trip to Disney World I remember in the early 90's. It was from pics from that trip that reminded me just how cool the Who Framed Roger Rabbit area at MGM Studios (aka Hollywood Studios) was and how bad my hair looked in the 90's.

Finally to my best friend and the person who makes my life magical, my husband Joe. His patience, ability to keep me from overthinking everything, and willingness to have Disney World be our vacation spot is what makes these books possible.

About the Author

Trisha Daab is an author, mom/not-so-evil stepmom, and food lover. She is the author of multiple books about Disney World: *Tasting the Magic from A-Z: The Best Food and Beverages at Walt Disney World*; *The Not-So-Evil Stepmother in the Most Magical Place on Earth: Planning Your Walt Disney World Family Vacation*; and a series of guides called *The Story Comes Alive* that help people experience their favorite Disney movies and characters, often in unexpected ways, at Walt Disney World.

Trisha has been visiting Disney since the 1980s, when she took first trip at 3 years old. (We won't talk about the VERY embarrassing picture of Trisha, in all of her coke-bottle-glasses-and-90's-hair glory, posing with Chewbacca, the only character whose hair could compete.)

Writing books about Disney World has been the perfect excuse to visit the parks more frequently, eat a lot of Disney food, and get new pictures with Chewy.

According to her sons and husband, she takes altogether too many pictures at Disney. You can see a lot of these pics, find out more about her, get updates on her next book, and see that epic 90's hair on Instagram @notsoevil_disneystepmom and on Facebook @authorTrishaDaab

Other books in the Story Comes Alive series:

Volume 2
DISNEY PRINCESSES AND FROZEN

The 11 official Disney princesses and their feature films and the movie *Frozen*. Available spring/summer 2019.

Volume 3
DISNEY CLASSICS & DISNEY PARKS AUTHENTIC

Movies and characters from the 1930-1990s that are NOT a member of the Fab Five, are a Disney princess, *Frozen*, Pixar, Star Wars, or Marvel. Also includes movies and characters that originated at Disney parks. Available summer 2019.

Volume 4
MODERN MAGIC AND PIXAR

Disney movies and characters from 2000 and beyond that are NOT a Disney Princess, Frozen, Star Wars or Marvel. Also includes the Pixar films. Available fall 2019.

Volume 5
STAR WARS AND MARVEL

Available late fall 2019.

Be the first to know when new volumes are available from Theme Park Press by following me on:

- Instagram @notsoevil_disneystepmom
- Facebook @authorTrishaDaab

ABOUT THEME PARK PRESS

Theme Park Press publishes books primarily about the Disney company, its history, culture, films, animation, and theme parks, as well as theme parks in general.

Our authors include noted historians, animators, Imagineers, and experts in the theme park industry.

We also publish many books by first-time authors, with topics ranging from fiction to theme park guides.

And we're always looking for new talent. If you'd like to write for us, or if you're interested in the many other titles in our catalog, please visit:

www.ThemeParkPress.com

• •

Theme Park Press Newsletter

Subscribe to our free email newsletter and enjoy:

- ◆ Free book downloads and giveaways
- ◆ Access to excerpts from our many books
- ◆ Announcements of forthcoming releases
- ◆ Exclusive additional content and chapters
- ◆ And more good stuff available nowhere else

To subscribe, visit www.ThemeParkPress.com, or send email to newsletter@themeparkpress.com.

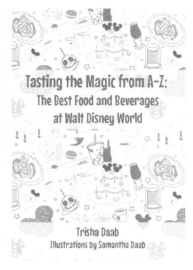

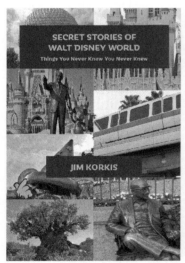

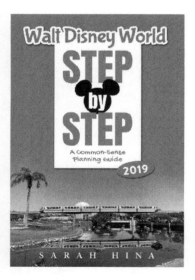

Read more about these books
and our many other titles at:

www.ThemeParkPress.com

Printed in Great Britain
by Amazon